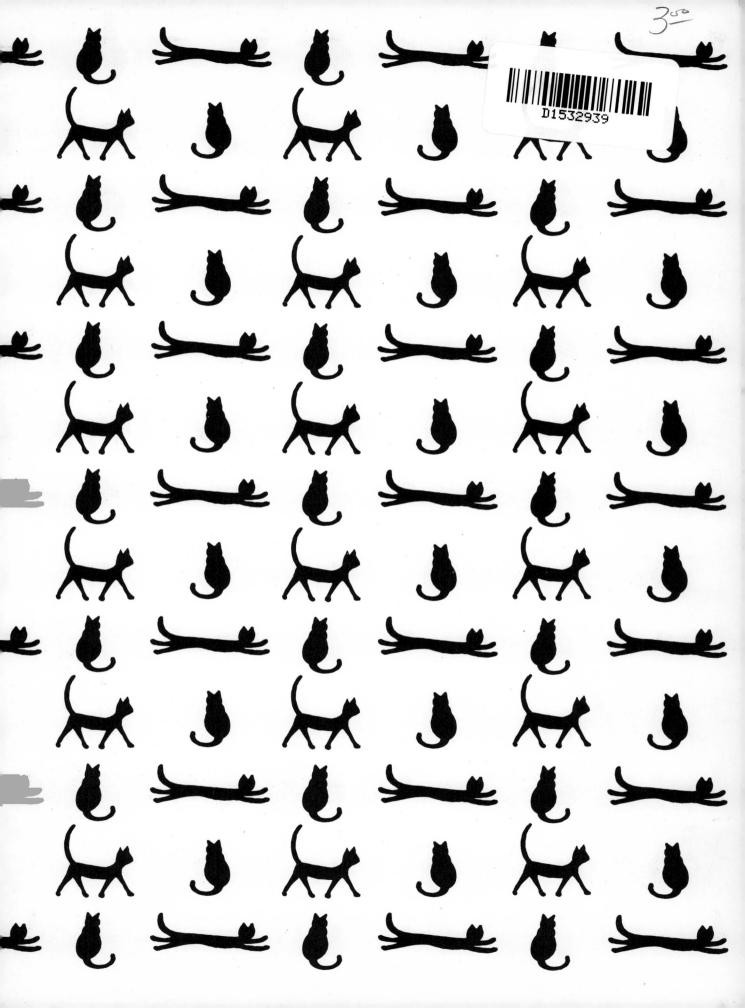

Pamela Peake's Catcraft

Pamela Peake was born in New Zealand
and trained as a zoologist
at Victoria University and Glasgow University.
She has published several best-selling books on toymaking:
Creative Soft Toy Making,
How to make Dinosaurs and Dragons and
The Complete Book of Soft Dolls,
as well as numerous articles
for magazines and journals.
Her work has been widely exhibited
throughout Britain and abroad.
Pamela Peake now lives in Kent with her family,
where she is a tutor
at various local Adult Education Colleges.
She also regularly demonstrates and lectures
on toymaking for several organisations.

Pamela Peake's Catcraft

COLLINS

First published in 1984
by William Collins Sons & Co Ltd
London · Glasgow · Sydney
Auckland · Johannesburg

© Pamela Peake, 1984

ISBN 0 00 411679 8

Typeset in Cheltenham Book
by John Swain & Son (Glasgow) Ltd

Colour origination by Intercrom S.A., Madrid
Printed and bound in Spain
by Graficromo, S.A., Cordoba

Acknowledgements

I AM SINCERELY GRATEFUL TO ALL those people who contributed information and ideas: to the students of Tonbridge and Sevenoaks Adult Centres who helped to test out many of the articles and so cheerfully encouraged me with their criticisms and suggestions: to Doreen Cuthbert and Audrey Pearce for loaning the Puss in the Corner Quilt and Cat's Cradle Bag respectively to be photographed: to Peggy Barnes for always being there when I wanted to talk over an idea: to Jan Dartnell and Wilma Picton for typing the manuscript.

Lastly I should like to thank my family and Cathy Gosling and Joan Clibbon of Collins who were very supportive and patient while this book was slowly taking shape.

Ightham, Kent 1983

Contents

Introduction 15

CHAPTER ONE

A Kindle of Kittens 19

Blue-eyed White Shorthair 19
Red Colourpoint Longhair 22
Red Tabby Shorthair 23
Japanese Bobtail 24
Blue Kitten 26
Seal Point Siamese 26
Ebony Oriental Shorthair 28
Sweet Dreams 28

CHAPTER TWO

Playtime Cats 30

Tom 30
Tabitha 34
Miss Pussy Willow 36

CHAPTER THREE

Patchwork Pets 41

Log Cabin Pot Holder 41
Cathedral Window Pincushion 43
Dresden Plate Egg Cosies 44
Catch Us If You Can Quilt 45
Siamese Kit Bag 48
Puss in the Corner 50
Cat's Cradle 52
More American Block Patterns 54
Egyptian Cat 56

CHAPTER FOUR

Cats to Quilt and Appliqué   59

Daisy Chain Quilt   59
The Owl and The Pussycat   62
A Touch of Nostalgia   65

CHAPTER FIVE

Cats to Embroider   69

The Gingham Collection   69
A Pair of Boxes   73
Cat in Clover   76

CHAPTER SIX

Cats to Wind, Crochet and Knit   80

Pompom Puss   80
Boots   82
Coiled Cat   86
Marmalade Moggy   88
Mittens of Kittens   90

CHAPTER SEVEN

The Big Cats   93

Tiger Cub   93
Velvet Lion   95
Tiger Tiger   97

CHAPTER EIGHT

Tail Piece   101

Duncan and Hamish   101
Margaret and Flora   105

List of Colour Plates

A Kindle of Kittens
(opposite page 32)

Playtime Cats
(opposite page 33)

Patchwork Pets
(opposite page 48)

Cats to Quilt and Appliqué
(opposite page 49)

Cats to Embroider
(opposite page 64)

Cats to Wind, Crochet and Knit
(opposite page 65)

The Big Cats
(opposite page 96)

Tail Piece
(opposite page 97)

Photographs by Graham Lees

Introduction

CATS HAVE ENJOYED A LONG AND close association with man but even so they still retain a streak of independence. The millions of strays around the world clearly demonstrate how well they are able to fend for themselves.

Man's relationship with domesticated animals usually centres on their usefulness as a ready source of food or as hunting companions and it is in this latter capacity that the Egyptians were possibly first attracted to cats. Indeed, all our early knowledge of cats as hunters and as domestic pets comes from Egypt. Whether cats were domesticated earlier elsewhere is unknown. Certainly the Egyptians appear to have been the only people to use cats as hunters for flushing wildfowl out of the reeds.

From about 1800 BC, the cat was well established in Egypt as a favoured pet enjoying the full protection of the law. Such adulation eventually led to the cat being worshipped and a definite cat culture became identified with the cat-headed goddess, Bast. This cult lasted for approximately 2000 years before it was finally banned in AD 390.

Bast was the goddess of motherhood, fertility and to a certain extent of moon worship. She was endowed with nine lives through association with the cat, a mystical divinity. Nine is also a mystical number being a trinity of trinities. The saying 'To have kittens' comes from a widespread superstition amongst women who were having a difficult labour. It can be traced back to very early times. All too often the women had a genuine fear that they would give birth to kittens – such was the power of superstition connected with the cat. Nowadays the saying is still used of an event with an element of apprehension and fear.

The Egyptians had a careful breeding programme for their pets, choosing good-natured individuals for mating. Both household pets and temple cats alike were given a burial and usually mummified when they died. From cat burials we know that the African Wild Cat was the first animal domesticated; even though some specimens of the Jungle Cat were probably also involved. The African Wild Cat extended all over Asia. The domesticated variety was either transported to China or the whole process was repeated there again. Household pets in the Far East enjoyed the same sort of popularity as those in Europe, being much valued by farmers.

The cat eventually reached Europe when the Romans copied some of the Egyptian religious cults, including cat worship. They also valued its ability to catch moles and mice. As the Roman Empire expanded the Romans took the cat with them. It is possible that it interbred with the European Wild Cat, which is darker in colour with more striking tabby markings than the African Wild Cat. Much later on the cat was spread to all corners of the world by European navigators and has since become virtually as cosmopolitan as man himself.

Perhaps it was because the cat figured so prominently in many pagan religions that the Christian church in the Middle Ages felt it necessary to persecute it. Cats were linked with devil worship and black cats in particular were considered to be witches in disguise. Hence they were hunted out and burnt, as were witches. Consequently it is quite easy to see how black cats came to be considered as unlucky in contrast to the more widespread and older association of good luck.

The cat now figures so prominently in our folk culture that its very presence in our daily life is for many synonymous with home comfort and security. Some would even go so far as to say that the cat cleverly adopted man as much as we domesticated it. Frequently they both share the same house, each with their own entrance – the human being the door and the cat the door flap, which was invented by Isaac Newton as long ago as the seventeenth century.

Cat shows introduced during the nineteenth century encouraged owners to take pride in their pets and to experiment with body form, colour and hair types. Thus the cat moved from the farmyard and kitchen to the drawing room. This elevation in status was initiated by the observations of Louis Pasteur, of vaccine fame, that cats were fastidiously clean and 'germ free'. Today there are over 100 recognised varieties of domestic cat which include the familiar Shorthairs, Longhairs, Siamese, Manx and Abyssinian cats as well as the unusual hairless and curly-coated varieties and the more exotic types. Even so, because cats have lived more independently of man and for a shorter time than other domesticated animals, they do not exhibit the enormous range seen in dogs.

With such a colourful history to draw on it is little wonder that images of the cat have been captured by artists and craftsmen for centuries and have been presented in virtually every kind of medium. Equally cats have inspired writers, poets, musicians, choreographers and more recently the film and television industry.

Puss in Boots was amongst the earliest of all literary cats, first appearing in print in 1697. Essentially a fairy tale with no readily discernible moral, Puss in Boots has lasting quality and is just as popular today as a much loved pantomime star. Dick Whittington's cat is another present-day pantomime star, but here the story is based on imperfectly remembered fourteenth century fact. Another notable character is Lewis Carroll's Cheshire Cat from *Alice in Wonderland*. His famous grin ensures that generations of children will be familiar with him. And who could possibly forget those rhymes learnt in the nursery about the Owl and the Pussycat or the Cat and the Fiddle?

It must be obvious that this book is for enthusiasts who love cats in all their manifestations. They may remember nostalgically a friend from their childhood, or already have a cat curled up on the rug in front of the fire or simply be besotted with them. I hope you will all enjoy making the articles in this book, whether practical or decorative, and perhaps your cat will even approve of the results. However, if you are 'only' a needleworker looking for a theme then there is a wide range of techniques and ideas for you to experiment with and maybe you too could become a felinophile!

CHAPTER ONE

A Kindle of Kittens

Baby animals always seem to have a special appeal of their own and these Kittens are no exception. The patterns represent the two principal body types and with careful selection of fur for both length of pile and colour you will be able to make Kittens for most of the popular breeds.

Blue-eyed White Shorthair

THIS KITTEN CONFORMS TO THE requirements for the British type and is described as cobby. The head is large and round with lovely deep blue sapphire eyes while the sturdy body is low on the legs, with broad shoulders and rump and a short tail.

Materials

30.5 cm (12 in) by 76 cm (30 in) wide white, unpolished short pile fur
170 g (6 oz) stuffing
pair 16 mm blue safety eyes
embroidery thread for nose and mouth
white felt for ear linings
whiskers optional

Measurements

Kitten stands 18 cm (7 in) tall from front paws to tip of ears.

To Make Up

Prepare a set of card patterns from the pattern grid and in addition cut a piece of card measuring 25.5 cm (10 in) by 12.5 cm (5 in) for the tail. Lay pattern on back of fur with all arrows matching the stroke of the fur (the direction of the pile) and draw round all pieces with a soft pencil, then cut out. The stroke of the fur will also lie down the length of the tail. Be careful to cut backing of fur only and not the pile. Cut a pair of ear linings from the white felt. A 6 mm ($\frac{1}{4}$ in) seam allowance is included in the pattern.

Start by making the darts on both side body pieces. Bring edges of mouth darts together and sew from X to Y, then bring together both Ys of the neck dart and sew from X through Y to X. Now make the chest dart on the underbody by bringing As together and sewing from X to A.

With right sides together, sew side bodies from C to A and then insert head gusset and sew from C to D on each side in turn. Close lower part of back below opening to B. Now position underbody matching A to A, and sew from A around front leg, then hind leg to B on each side in turn. Clip the seam allowance at the turn between front and hind legs to release the tension. Turn completed skin right side out and insert a handful of stuffing into the head.

Place eyes against head and move them around until you find the correct position. Resist the temptation to place them too high. When satisfied with the position, pierce a hole for each eye with a knitting needle. This hole must be just large enough to fit the shank of the eye. Remove stuffing from head and turn skin inside out. If a knitted rather than a woven fur is used for the kitten then there is a real

19

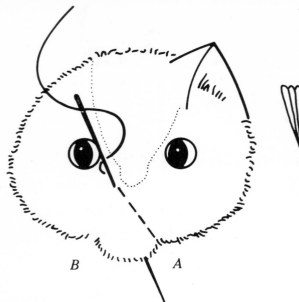

Figure 1.1

Face shaping. The stitch needed to sink in the other eye starts under the chin at B.

Figure 1.2

Embroider nose with satin stitch. Work straight stitches closely together across the nose area being careful to keep the edges even. Finish with long stitches in the centre. Then bring needle out at A and pass in at B leaving long thread slack on the surface. Bring needle out at C, looping slack behind and pulling up tight on the excess thread before passing needle back into head at D (base of nose) to complete the mouth. Fasten off.

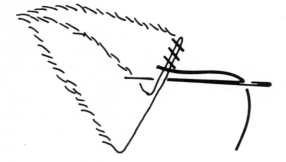

Figure 1.3

Fold ear with raw edges even then whip together by oversewing along edge.

possibility that the threads around the hole may unravel or stretch and the eyes may well pull free from the toy. The solution to this problem is to glue a felt patch in place on the inside of the head. A hole can then be pierced through the felt for the eye shank.

Turn skin right side out and fix eyes in place with their safety washers. Further shaping to the face can be achieved by anchoring a strong thread at A and taking the needle up to the inside corner of the eye and catching a small stitch before returning needle to A, as in Figure 1.1. By pulling on the thread, the cheeks and nose will be thrown forward and the eyes drawn back into the head.

Use all six strands of embroidery thread to work a satin stitch triangular shaped nose. Choose a light flesh colour in preference to black. Follow Figure 1.2 to work the mouth.

Sew a felt ear lining to a fur piece, leaving the base open. Turn right side out and release

any fur trapped in the seam. Now fold ear in half and whip all four raw edges together, Figure 1.3. Position ear on side of head and ladder stitch in place. Work 6 mm ($\frac{1}{4}$ in) up from base, thus spreading the ear and shortening it. Make second ear in same way.

Fold tail in half lengthways and sew down the long side, in the direction of the pile, that is with the stroke of the fur, and across the short end. Turn right side out. Fold tail in half lengthways again with the seam lying in the groove, as in Figure 1.4, and ladder stitch the folded edges together. After working a few stitches, pull up on thread to curl the tail. Sew finished tail to body at B.

Decide whether your kitten needs whiskers. This will depend on whether the toy is for a young child and therefore likely to need washing. The whiskers on all the kittens have been made with nylon fishing line. Choose a suitable colour of nylon to match your fur and

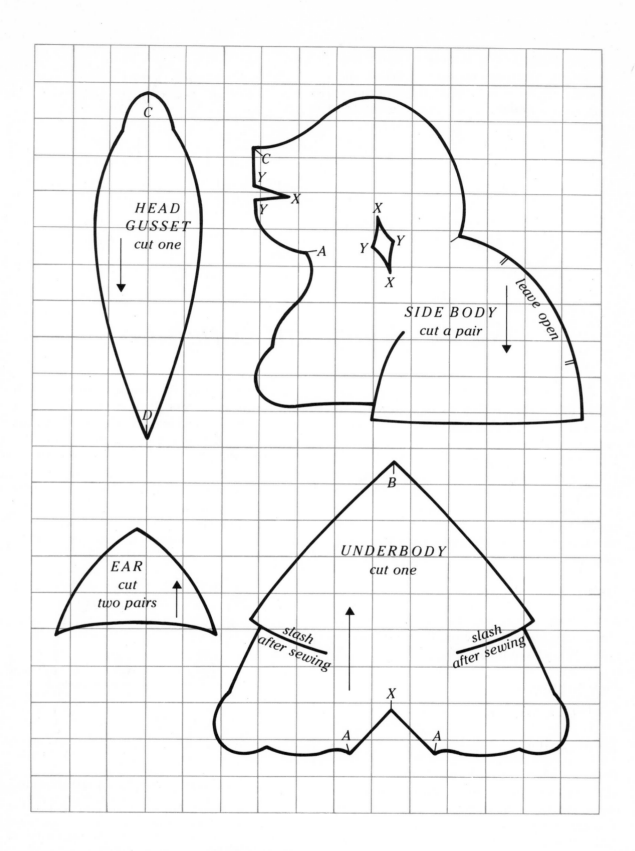

HEAD GUSSET
cut one

SIDE BODY
cut a pair

leave open

EAR
cut
two pairs

UNDERBODY
cut one

slash
after sewing

slash
after sewing

Pattern grid. Blue-eyed White Shorthair and
Red Colourpoint Longhair Kittens one square=2.5 cm (1 in)

21

also watch out for the thickness of the monofilament which is measured by its test or breaking strength. Whiskers need to be tied into the fur if they are not to spring free and Figure 2.1 shows how to make the Half Blood Knots which are the most suitable for toy making.

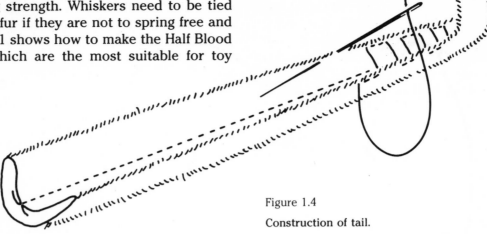

Figure 1.4
Construction of tail.

Red Colourpoint Longhair

COLOURPOINT LONGHAIR CATS ARE the direct result of experiments to establish a Siamese-patterned cat with Persian coat and body type. By using the pattern for either the White Shorthair or Red Tabby Kitten with a white or cream long pile fur and shading the points, you will have a colourpoint kitten. These same kittens are known as Himalayans in North America. Leave off the shading and you will have the more familiar Persian.

Materials

As for Blue-eyed White Shorthair but use long pile cream fur with cream felt ear linings ordinary rust colour pencil

Measurements

As for Blue-eyed White Shorthair

To Make Up

Prepare a set of card patterns from the pattern grid for Blue-eyed White Shorthair Kitten (page 21). Tail should measure 20 cm (8 in) by 12.5 cm (5 in). Make up the body by following instructions already given, insert eyes, stuff body and close opening. Make and attach the shorter tail.

Sink a stitch on the inside corner of each eye to throw the cheeks forward. The fur on the nose bridge will need to be shaved shorter by careful cutting with embroidery scissors following the pile of the fur to keep it smooth. Further shaping can then be given to the face by needle modelling along the head gusset immediately behind the nose and working back to the eyes, Figure 1.5. Finish by embroidering the nose and inserting whiskers.

Figure 1.5

Further shaping can be achieved by raising the bridge of the nose. Starting with thread in gusset seam at upper right corner of nose, pass needle through head horizontally to gusset seam on the left. Take a small stitch and pass needle back to the right side. Continue like this working slowly back towards the eyes and pulling up on thread as each stitch is made, thus raising the bridge. Diagram shows stitching nearly completed.

Sew ear linings to ears leaving base open. Turn right side out and tuck in the base to make the ears shorter. Whip edges together, without folding in half but pull up on the thread to curve the ears slightly. Sew ears in place on outside corners of head.

At this stage you will have made a self-colour Persian and it only remains to colour the points in order to have a colourpoint Longhair instead. You can use any of the colours that are found on Siamese cats. This Kitten has been coloured on the nose, cheeks, paws, edge of ears and tip of tail by stroking a dampened pencil along the pile until the required depth of colour is obtained.

Red Tabby Shorthair

ALL THE SHORTHAIR GINGER AND marmalade cats with their various shadings mixing with the ground colour are in fact Red Tabby Shorthairs. The true pedigree should be a rich, deep orange-red with even darker markings and have hazel or orange eyes.

Materials

61 cm (24 in) wide by 46 cm (18 in) long ginger, polished short pile fur
170 g (6 oz) stuffing
pair 16 mm hazel safety eyes
embroidery thread for nose and mouth
colour pencil for tabby markings

Measurements

Kitten stands 20 cm (8 in) tall to tip of ear and has an overall length of 30 cm (12 in).

To Make Up

Prepare a set of card patterns from the pattern grid (page 25) and in addition cut one piece of card measuring 25.5 cm (10 in) by 30.5 cm (12 in) for the body and another 25.5 cm (10 in) by 12.5 cm (5 in) for the tail.

Lay pattern on back of fur and draw round all pieces with a soft pencil, then cut out. The stroke of the fur lies down the length of the tail and also with the long side of the body. Mark the centre point of each short end of the body

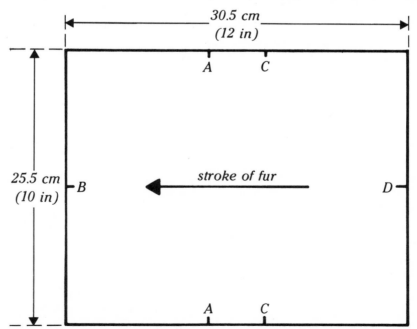

Figure 1.6

Red Tabby Shorthair body pattern showing position of markings.
B and D are the centre points of each short side.

A and C are the same distance from the corner as B and D respectively.
The distance between A and C on each side is 5 cm (2 in).

and the paired side marks A and C as in Figure 1.6.

Now take a corner of the body between B and A and with right sides together fold it diagonally to bring A and B together as in Figure 1.7. Sew, rounding off the point. Bring second A to AB by folding the other corner diagonally and again sew. Make the front legs in the same way by bringing D and Cs together. Turn right side out through AC opening, stuff firmly then close.

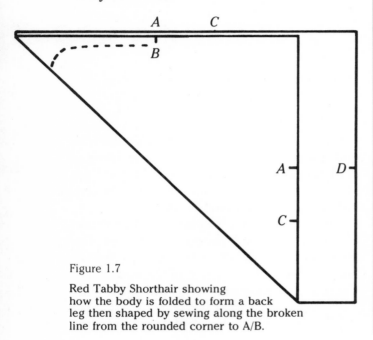

Figure 1.7

Red Tabby Shorthair showing how the body is folded to form a back leg then shaped by sewing along the broken line from the rounded corner to A/B.

Make tail by following instructions for Blue-eyed White Shorthair Kitten and when finished sew in place.

This little Kitten has pouched cheeks that are formed by easing the long side of the cheek dart to fit the short side before bringing Y to Y and sewing Y to X. Make darts on top of head by closing and again sewing Y to X. Now place right sides of head together and sew from A to B. Insert gusset matching A to A and sew from A to C on each side in turn.

Turn head right side out and insert eyes, stuff firmly then run a strong gathering thread around neck opening pulling up to draw the edges together. Position head on body and ladder stitch securely in place.

Make ears by sewing pairs together leaving bottom edges open. Turn right sides out, clean seams by releasing any trapped pile then whip open edges together. Sew each ear in place as for Red Colourpoint.

Embroider a triangular shaped block of satin stitches for the nose and then work a mouth immediately beneath. The bridge of the nose may be raised by taking stitches through from side to side.

Finally, use a colour pencil to mark on tabby bands. If you have chosen a rich ginger colour fur to begin with, these markings will not show up clearly and it might just be that you have made a Red Self Shorthair Kitten instead!

Japanese Bobtail

THIS IS AN ANCIENT BREED UNLIKE any other because it has a short curved tail and the body is neither foreign nor cobby. In no way is the Bobtail related to the Manx and Stumpies. Coat colour is traditionally tricoloured, that is black, red and white, and the pattern must be formed with distinctly separated patches.

Materials

Small pieces of red, black and white unpolished short pile fur
170 g (6 oz) stuffing
pair of 16 mm green safety cats' eyes
apricot thread for nose
whiskers

Measurements

The Bobtail Kitten is slightly shorter than Red Tabby.

To Make Up

Cut a set of paper patterns for head, body and gusset. Decide where you want patches of colour to be and cut paper pattern accordingly to these areas. Label each piece carefully with its colour and position in relation to other pieces. Each paper piece must now be made into a card pattern and a 6 mm ($\frac{1}{4}$ in) seam allowance must be added on to all new cut edges, Figure 1.8.

Cut ears and tail from black fur. The tail should measure 12.5 cm (5 in) square. Cut out other pieces according to choice then sew them together into complete body, head and gusset piece. Assemble as given for Red Tabby. After sewing on tail, curve it over to touch the body and sew in place so that you have a tight bob.

To finish, omit the raised nose bridge but give the Bobtail whiskers. Pay particular attention to grooming making sure that all seams are free from trapped fur.

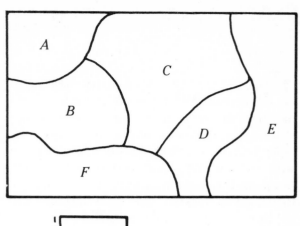

Figure 1.8

Diagram of body pattern showing a possible layout for Japanese Bobtail Kitten. Section E is shown with the new seam allowance indicated by broken line. Sequence for joining would be B to A – C to A/B – D to C – E to C/D – F to B/C/D. Avoid sharp angles and joins within darts. Also remember to carry same colour over from head on to head gusset.

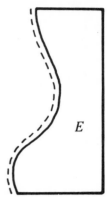

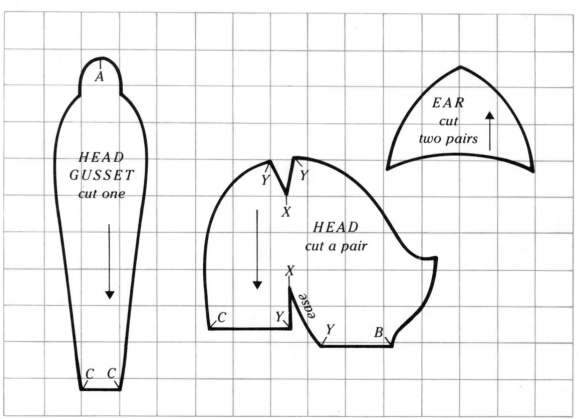

Pattern grid. Red Tabby Shorthair, Japanese Bobtail and Blue Kitten one square=2.5 cm (1 in)

Blue Kitten

BLUE TO CAT BREEDERS MEANS A bluish grey and is in effect a dilute form of black. There should be no tabby markings, shading or traces of white hair anywhere. Most breeds of cats have blue forms, some with copper eyes and others with green. Amongst the more well known blues are the British Blue, Russian Blue, Blue Burmese and the Korat. This particular little Kitten does not belong to any recognisable breed so I have simply called it a Blue Kitten.

Materials

As for Red Tabby Shorthair but use a silky grey fur instead
pair of 16 mm green safety cats' eyes

Measurements

Kitten measures 18 cm (7 in) from nose to back legs.

To Make Up

Cut head and tail as for Red Tabby (page 25) and a piece of card 25.5 cm (10 in) square for the body.

Follow instructions for Red Tabby to make up but note that there will be no opening AC. In order to turn the completed body skin right side out you will have to make a slit that will later be hidden by the head, Figure 1.9. Because this is a shorter body, be careful to position the head forward rather than up on the back.

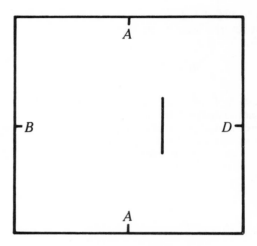

Figure 1.9

Blue Kitten body pattern showing position of neck opening slit behind front legs at D.

Seal Point Siamese

OF ALL THE MANY DIFFERENT breeds of cat the Siamese is the most recognisable with its distinctive patterning. The body is long and sleek and the head wedge-shaped – quite unlike the cobby form of the previous Kittens. In addition the ears should be large, wide at the bottom and pointed at the top while the eyes should be a deep blue and slanted. Many stories abound about the origin of the Siamese but there seems no doubt that it was already a well established variety in Ayudha, the ancient capital of Siam.

Materials

60 cm (23½ in) square of cream, short pile polished fur
170 g (6 oz) stuffing
pair 16 mm blue safety eyes
dark brown embroidery thread
brown pencil
whiskers optional

Measurements

Kitten measures 15 cm (6 in) to tip of ears and approximately 40 cm (16 in) long from front paws to tip of tail.

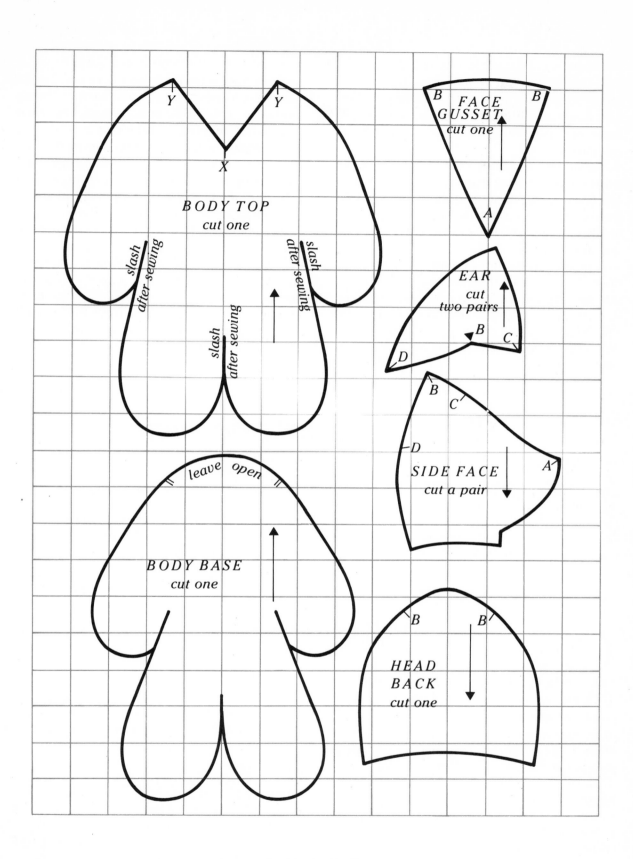

Pattern grid. Seal Point Siamese and
Ebony Oriental Shorthair one square=2.5 cm (1 in)

To Make Up

Prepare a set of card patterns from the pattern grid (page 27). Cut a piece for the tail by following instructions for first White Shorthair Kitten. Draw round pattern and cut out in same way. A 6 mm ($\frac{1}{4}$ in) seam is allowed for on pattern.

Make dart on body top by bringing Ys together and sewing from X to Y. Sew base to top, leaving an opening. Slash hind legs free from body then turn skin right side out, stuff firmly and close. Make tail following Figure 1.4 and sew to Kitten at Y.

Sew ears together in pairs round outer curved edges, turn right side out. Place short straight edge BC to BC on matching side face and sew in place. Clip seam allowance at B and turn long edge BD down against BD on face and again sew in place. Sew second ear in place on other side.

Now sew face gusset in place from A to B on each side in turn, then close seam from nose at A down to neck edge. Check that bases of ears are securely caught in the seams before moving on. Sew head back to face being careful to match B to B in both places. Turn completed head right side out.

Determine where you want the eyes to be then fix them in place. Stuff head firmly, draw up neck opening with a gathering thread and fasten off. Place head on body so that it sits over the front legs and ladder stitch in place. Attach whiskers if required and embroider the nose.

The characteristic patterning is achieved by stroking a dampened pencil along the stroke of the fur. Proceed cautiously, colouring a little at a time until the desired effect is achieved and remember that points are usually lighter coloured on Kittens.

Ebony Oriental Shorthair

SIAMESE CATS WITH ALL-OVER colouring have been known for a very long time. Technically they are the same breed but for show purposes are called variously Oriental, Foreign and even Havana.

Use the Seal Point Siamese pattern and instructions to make this Kitten, substituting black fur and green eyes. Work the nose in black embroidery thread and line the ears with black felt.

Sweet Dreams

AS PLAYFUL AS THEY ARE, YOUNG Kittens like most young animals need plenty of rest and this cushion, using a cat print, makes an ideal bed to lay in the bottom of the basket. The polybead filling keeps it lightweight, warm, cosy and easy to clean.

Materials

1 m (1 yd) of 115 cm (45 in) wide catprint cotton
33 cm (13 in) of 91 cm (36 in) wide wadding
14 pints of polybeads

Measurements

This oval shaped cushion measures approximately 43 cm (17 in) by 56 cm (22 in).

To Make Up

Figure 1.10 shows how to cut sides, top and base from the print fabric. In addition you will need to cut a base and top from wadding.

Baste the large piece of wadding to the wrong side of the base fabric and likewise the smaller piece of wadding to the top fabric.

Sew a short end of both side pieces together to make a long strip, then sew remaining short ends together but this time leave a 5 cm (2 in) opening in the middle of the seam. Run a row of gathering stitches around both the top and the bottom edges of the side and pull up to fit the base and top ovals respectively. Distribute the gathers evenly then sew in place. Turn cushion skin right side out and fill with polybeads until you achieve the desired degree of firmness for your Kitten. Close the side seam opening with ladder stitch.

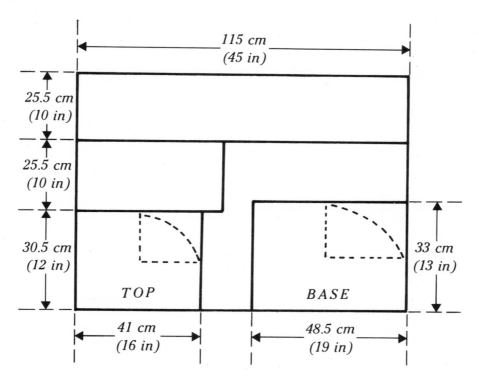

Figure 1.10

Measurements and layout for cutting sides, top and bottom of cat bed. Prepare an oval for the top by folding the rectangle in half, twice, so that it is quartered. Cut an arc to form the largest oval possible within the given area. Cut an oval for the base in the same way.

CHAPTER TWO

Playtime Cats

Here are three cats that will each provide many hours of fun for their young owners. Tom, the black cat, is a very robust knockabout character who will stand up to much hard play as will Tabitha, the more gentle looking striped cat. Miss Pussy Willow has been designed especially for children who delight in dressing their toys.

Tom

THE PRESENT DAY POPULARITY OF black cats as bringers of good luck is in direct contrast to their medieval image of deepest suspicion when they were associated with witchcraft. Tom is a typical British shorthair cat with deep body, full chest, short thick tail and lovely large yellow eyes.

Materials

50 cm (19 in) of 140 cm (54 in) wide short pile, unpolished black fur
454 g (1 lb) stuffing
pair 18 mm yellow safety cats' eyes
nylon fishing line for whiskers
embroidery thread for nose

Measurements

Tom measures 61 cm (24 in) from front paws to tip of tail.

To Make Up

Make a set of card patterns from the pattern grids (pages 31 and 32). A 6 mm ($\frac{1}{4}$ in) seam allowance is included on pattern pieces. Lay pattern on back of fur fabric with arrows matching the stroke of fur (direction of pile). Draw round pattern with a light coloured pencil or chalk. Cut out all pieces being careful to cut pairs where necessary instead of two.

Body: Make dart in each outer hind leg by bringing A to A and sewing from X to A. Sew a hind leg on to side body from B through A to C and repeat on the other side.

Sew body gussets together from G to H leaving the centre open. Sew inner hind legs to body gusset on each side matching D to D and E to E. Place one completed side body to matching body gusset and sew from E/C forward to D/B, then round front leg to F. Repeat on other side. Clip corner at F to release tension. Now position chest and sew first from F to F through G then on each side from F to M. Close centre back seam L to J.

Place J of tail to J at centre back and sew in place from K to J to K, then fold tail in half lengthways and sew edges together. Press base of tail flat and close opening between C through KHK to C.

Head: Make darts on both side heads by bringing Y to Y and sewing from X to Y. Sew head pieces together from nose at O down to the neck edge. Insert head gusset matching O to O and sew each side in turn back to neck edge. Take care to get correct shaping at nose even if it means slow handstitching on the seam allowance.

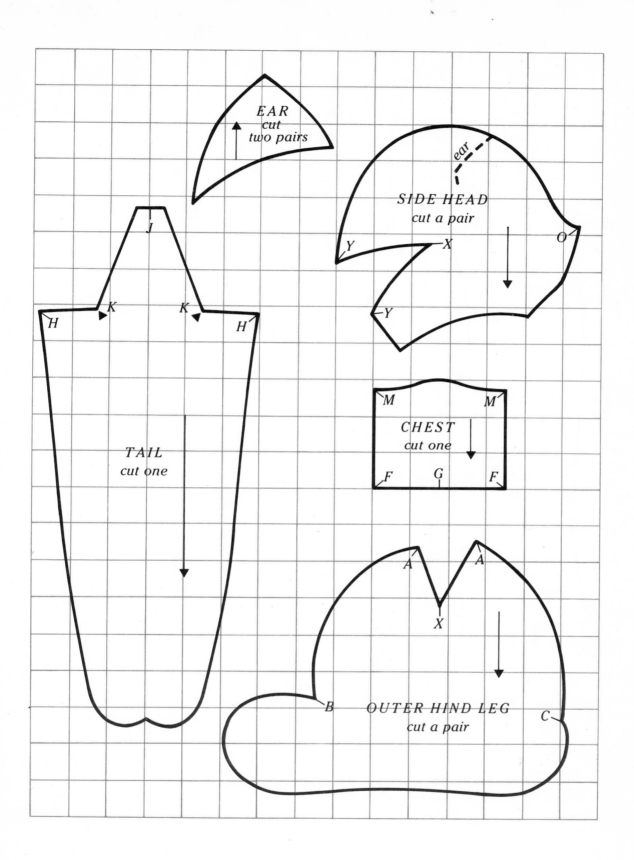

EAR
cut
two pairs

SIDE HEAD
cut a pair

ear

Y   X   O

Y

J

H   K   K   H

TAIL
cut one

M   M

CHEST
cut one

F   G   F

A   A

X

B   OUTER HIND LEG
cut a pair   C

Pattern grid. Tom one square=2.5 cm (1 in)

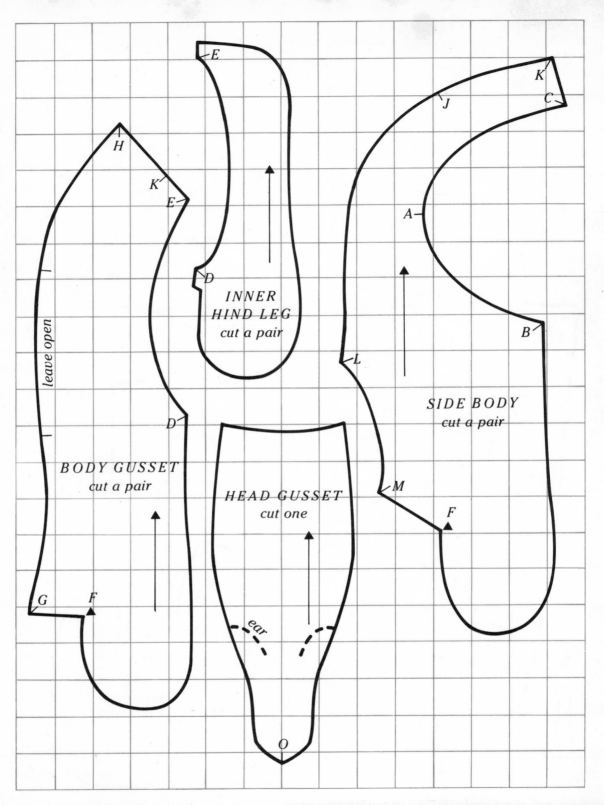

E

H

K

E

D

INNER HIND LEG
cut a pair

J

K

C

A

B

L

SIDE BODY
cut a pair

leave open

D

BODY GUSSET
cut a pair

HEAD GUSSET
cut one

M

F

G

F

ear

O

Pattern grid. Tom one square=2.5 cm (1 in)

A Kindle of Kittens (opposite)
On the chair: *Blue-eyed White Shorthair, Blue Kitten.*
On the cushion: *Japanese Bobtail, Red Colourpoint Longhair.*
On the floor: *Red Tabby Shorthair, Seal Point Siamese,
Ebony Oriental Shorthair.*

Turn completed head right side out and push through neck opening of body. Be careful to position the head correctly then sew in place by working a double line of stitches. Now turn completed fabric skin of cat right side out through body gusset opening. Insert safety eyes and then stuff the head firmly, followed by the tail which need not be so firm. Continue stuffing, front legs followed by hind legs and finally finish with the body. Close opening with ladder stitch.

Sew ears together in pairs and turn them right side out. Tuck in corners and whip bottom edges together. Position ears on head and ladder stitch each in place across the front first and then along the back.

To bring the nose forward you must take a strong thread up from the neck to the inside corner of an eye and then return it to the centre front seam about 12 mm ($\frac{1}{2}$ in) from the neck. Pull tightly on thread to sink eye into head and thus throw nose forward. Work another stitch on the inside corner of the second eye and again pull up tightly before fastening off. Using all six strands of em-broidery thread work a triangular shaped nose in satin stitch, then a mouth. The mouth should be positioned just under the nose.

Whiskers are optional and should be determined by the age of the child who will be playing with Tom. Nylon fishing line makes superb whiskers that will not become limp. To anchor nylon thread into the head you must work Half Blood knots rather than stitches which would spring free, Figure 2.1. Thread a needle with 30 cm (12 in) of line then take a small stitch through the fur at the side of the nose. Wind the needle end over the other end at least four times then insert needle through bottom loop and pull firmly. This will draw the knot tight to the base and result in two whiskers. Work a total of four whiskers on each side and two above each eye. Trim all whiskers to required length keeping those above the eyes shorter than the rest.

Finish your toy by carefully grooming all the seams to release any trapped fur. You may like to make a collar for your cat or tie a colourful ribbon around the neck.

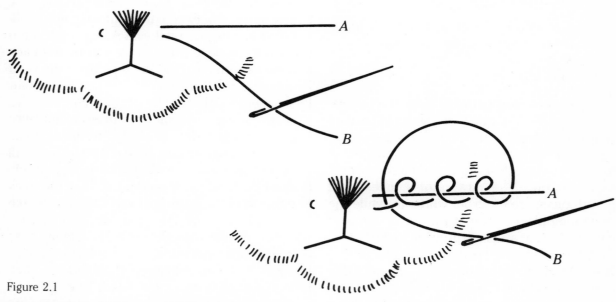

Figure 2.1

Construction of whiskers using nylon fishing line to tie Half Blood Knots. Thread nylon on needle and pass through head and back again to B, leaving short end at A. Take a small stitch on the other side of the head so that whiskers can be pulled up and sunk into fur. Wind B (needle end) over short end at least four times then pass needle between threads at base of loops and pull up tight, drawing loops down into a tight coil. Work whiskers on other side in same way. Trim to required length.

Playtime Cats (opposite)
Left to right: *Tom, Miss Pussy Willow, Tabitha.*

Tabitha

PROBABLY THE MOST POPULAR OF all domestic cats today is the Tabby which has an historical record stretching back over 4000 years to Egypt where it was domesticated. The name 'tabby' comes from Attabiy, a district in Baghdad, where for centuries a watered silk or taffeta was made that was similar to the colour and sheen of a Tabby cat.

Materials

50 cm (19 in) of 140 cm (54 in) wide short pile, unpolished grey fur
23 cm (9 in) by 53 cm (21 in) wide white fur
340 g (12 oz) stuffing
black and pink embroidery thread
small piece of old gold felt
pair 12 mm ($\frac{1}{2}$ in) black safety eyes or domed buttons
black pencil or marker pen

Measurements

Tabitha is 30.5 cm (12 in) tall and measures 61 cm (24 in) from front to tip of tail.

To Make Up

Make a set of card patterns from the pattern grid (page 35). A 6 mm ($\frac{1}{4}$ in) seam allowance is included on pattern pieces. Place pattern on wrong side of fur with arrows following pile of fur. Draw round the pattern with a soft pencil, then cut out. The paws, soles, chest and mouth piece are cut from white fur while the remaining pieces are cut from grey fur. You will need to cut a strip of grey fur 46 cm (18 in) long by 15 cm (6 in) wide for the tail.

Body: Start by sewing back paws to each side body and the underbody, matching A to A and B to B. Sew the two side bodies together down the centre back, leaving an opening for stuffing. Now sew the underbody to the side body down each front leg, matching C to C and D to D. Sew front paws in place again matching D to D. The sides and underbody may now be sewn together from the back of the front legs, round the back paws to the base of the centre back seam. Sew a sole to the base of each front paw, matching E to E. Insert chest, matching F to F, and sew.

Clip corners, then turn the completed skin right side out. Stuff through the neck opening and the centre back. Close back seam with ladder stitch. Run a gathering thread around the grey fur of the neck opening, draw up and fasten off. If the front legs splay outwards you will need to brace them together. Do this by pushing the legs inwards and ladder stitching the crease, so formed, at the inside top of each leg, to the underbody.

Fold the tail in half lengthways and sew along the stroke of the fur and across the short end. Turn right side out. Now fold tail in half lengthways again, this time enclosing the seam at the bottom of the fold. Ladder stitch the sides of the tail together, pulling up after every few stitches so that the tail curls. Sew tail to body.

Head: Sew the dart XY in both front and back head pieces. Insert the chin matching G to G, sew in place between the front and back head. Leave an opening on the back edge of the chin for turning head through. Sew front and back head together around the top edge from G on one side to G on the other. Turn head right side out. Cut circles of old gold felt to surround each eye and then insert safety eyes at this stage. If domed black buttons are used they are sewn on after the head is stuffed. Stuff head and close opening with ladder stitch. Position head on shoulders so that the neck opening of the body is covered. Ladder stitch securely in place.

Sew the ears together in pairs, leaving base open. Turn right side out and oversew bottom edges together. Fold ears in half and sew each in place on side of the head. The fold lies towards the crown. A more pleasing expression will be obtained if you take a strong thread from the lower edge of each ear and pull it through to the mouth area and then fasten off securely.

The third sole piece is used to make the cheeks. Turn under raw edges, evenly, to make an oval and hem. Sew in position on face

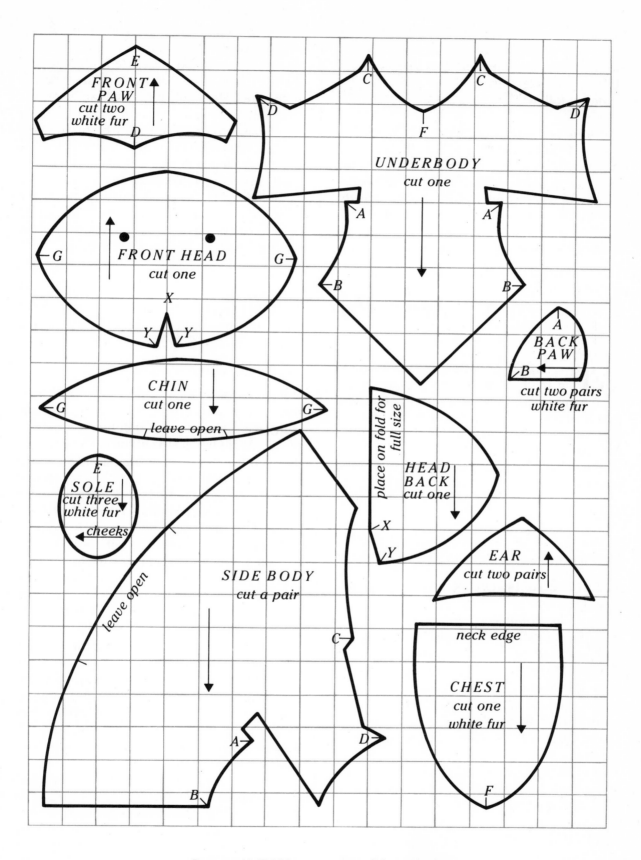

Pattern grid. **Tabitha one square=2.5 cm (1 in)**

covering the threads used to pull in the ears. Embroider a nose and mouth with pink thread. The nose is worked as a triangular block of satin stitches and the mouth as long, straight stitches. Whiskers are optional and could be made by following the instructions given for Tom.

Finishing and grooming: Work claw marks on the front paws with black straight stitches. These stitches pass over the paws and should be pulled in tight and tied off. Brush all seams to release trapped fur. Your cat is now ready to receive tabby markings. It is a wise precaution at this stage to test your choice of black, be it pen or pencil, on a scrap of fur.

Check that it does not react with the fur to give a bluish or purple tint and that it dries without clogging the fur. Now make a tabby patterning all over the grey fur, working both with and against the pile so that the colour is evenly distributed. Remember to mark an M on the forehead. Work small areas at a time, allowing ink or paint to dry thoroughly before moving on. Pencil is easiest in that it does not need to dry. When finished, give Tabitha a final, very gentle brushing. A toy made in this way is not suitable for a young child who might possibly want to suck and chew the fur. You would need to use black or ginger fur instead of grey and thus make a bicolour cat instead.

Miss Pussy Willow

MOST LITTLE GIRLS LOVE DRESSing their dolls and playing make believe games with them and many is the time that a family pet has been substituted for the doll and subjected to just this kind of play. Because Miss Pussy Willow is a toy cat, she will not spoil the game by jumping out of the pram.

Materials

50 cm (19 in) of 140 cm (54 in) wide long pile, silky grey fur
454 g (1 lb) stuffing
pair 16 mm green safety cats' eyes
pink embroidery thread for nose
61 cm (24 in) of 91 cm (36 in) wide pink cotton for underwear
157 cm (62 in) lace to trim underwear
1 m (39 in) narrow elastic
76 cm (30 in) of 91 cm (36 in) wide floral print for dress
1.5 m (58 in) lace to trim dress
small hank No 2 garden Raffia for bonnet
lace, ribbons and flowers to trim bonnet

Measurements

Miss Pussy Willow stands 48 cm (19 in) tall.

To Make Up

Make a set of card patterns for the body from the pattern grids (pages 37 and 39). A 6 mm ($\frac{1}{4}$ in) seam allowance is included on pattern pieces. Avoid having to cut the leg pieces from doubled fur by either making a full size card pattern to begin with or by drawing around the card pattern on the fur and then turning it over and drawing round the reverse half. Cut a piece of fur measuring 30.5 cm (12 in) long by 12.5 cm (5 in) wide for the tail.

Make a set of card patterns for the sleeves and bodice from the pattern grid. Measurements and a diagram for the skirt, petticoat and pantaloons are given in the text.

Body: Start by making all the darts on the body first, matching Ys to Ys and then sewing each dart in turn from X to Y. Make the darts on each arm piece in the same way, then sew arms together in pairs leaving the top open. Turn right side out and stuff nearly to the top. Now sew front body to back body enclosing an arm on each side. Leave the neck and base open. Turn right side out.

Prepare a leg by pulling Ds of foot apart to straighten out and match DED to corresponding letters on leg. Seam across. Fold leg in half lengthways and sew back leg seam from F to G. Insert sole matching F to F and easing fullness on the toes. Turn leg right

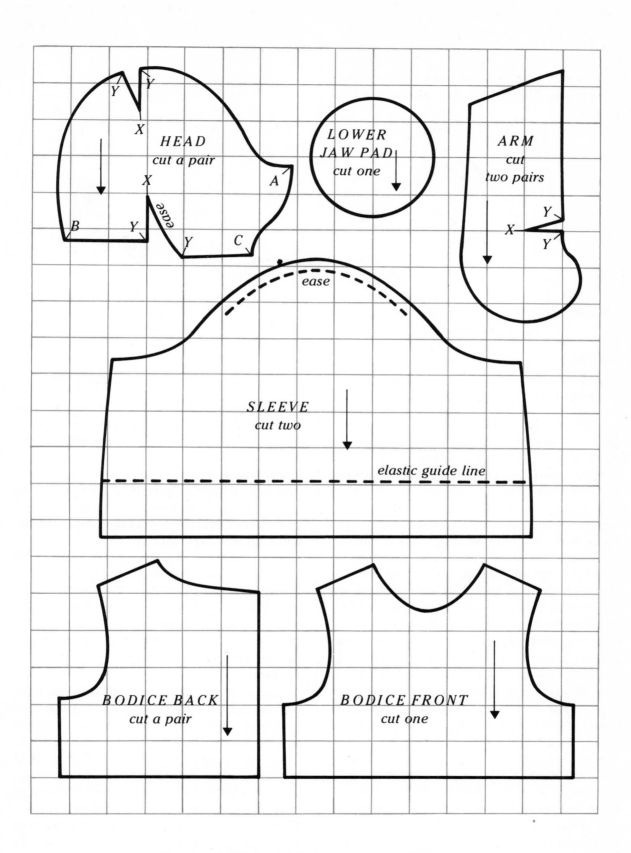

HEAD
cut a pair

LOWER
JAW PAD
cut one

ARM
cut
two pairs

ease

SLEEVE
cut two

elastic guide line

BODICE BACK
cut a pair

BODICE FRONT
cut one

Pattern grid. **Miss Pussy Willow** one square=2.5 cm (1 in)

37

side out and stuff nearly to the top. Baste in position on body front with right sides together and toes facing over the shoulder, Figure 2.2. Make second leg in same way. Stuff body firmly, turn in lower edge then ladder stitch across the bottom, securely enclosing the legs.

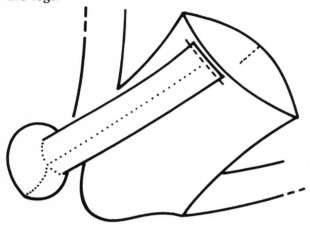

Figure 2.2

Miss Pussy Willow showing how leg is placed against front edge of body for basting in place.

Make the dart on the top of each head piece, then ease long side of each cheek dart to fit short side before sewing them. Sew head together from A to C then insert head gusset and sew each side in turn from A to B. Turn head right side out, determine best position for eyes then fix them in place. Stuff head firmly and gather up neck opening leaving a small opening that will fit on to the body.

Using a strong thread, take a stitch from under the chin up to the inside corner of an eye then back to start, pull up tight to sink the eye, then fasten off. Sink eye on other side in same way. Now gather outer edge of lower jaw pad and insert a ball of stuffing before pulling up. Shave pile of fur away from pad and try it against head for size. With some furs you may have to cut a smaller pad. If the size is right, ladder stitch the pad in place. Push head right down on to neck and sew head to body.

Sew ears together in pairs and turn right side out. Shave away the pile from the inside surface of each ear then whip the bottom edges together. Sew each ear in place with the front edge starting about 2.5 cm (1 in) above the eye and lying on the gusset seam while the back edge should curve down behind the eye.

Embroider a triangular shaped nose with satin stitches and work a mouth of straight stitches on the front top edge of the lower jaw pad, Figure 2.3.

Figure 2.3

Position of mouth and nose for Miss Pussy Willow.

To make the tail, follow the instructions given for Tabitha. When finished, sew in place just above the centre back dart on the bottom at T.

Underwear: Make a card pattern for the pantaloons from Figure 2.4, then cut two pieces from pink cotton. Sew the curved centre front seam first and then hem leg edges and trim with lace. Stretch a length of elastic across each leg in turn, about 5 cm (2 in) above lace, and zigzag in place. Now close centre back seam but leave an opening for the tail. Refold pantaloons to bring inside leg edges together and sew. Fold down a hem at the waist, large enough to act as an elastic casing, sew and insert elastic. Neaten tail opening.

Cut a piece of pink cotton measuring 30.5 cm (12 in) by 91 cm (36 in) for the petticoat. Sew two short sides together leaving an opening for the tail towards the top. Hem lower long edge and trim with lace. Fold down top edge and make a hem large enough to be an elastic casing. Sew, insert elastic and close opening. Neaten tail opening.

Dress: In addition to the card patterns already prepared for the sleeves and bodice you will need to cut a skirt measuring 33 cm (13 in) by

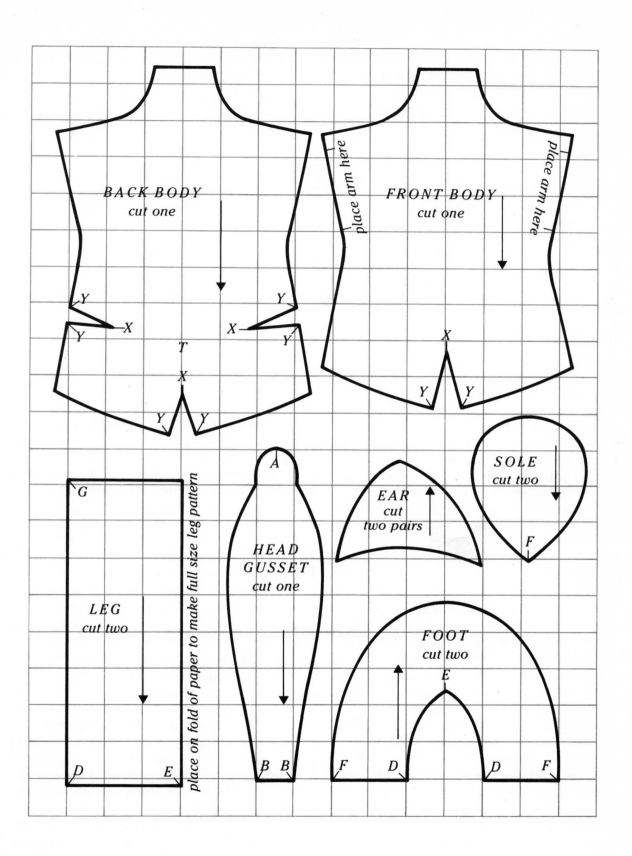

BACK BODY
cut one

FRONT BODY
cut one

place arm here

place arm here

Y

Y

X

X

Y

Y

X

T

X

Y

Y

Y

Y

G

LEG
cut two

D

E

place on fold of paper to make full size leg pattern

A

HEAD
GUSSET
cut one

B B

EAR
cut
two pairs

SOLE
cut two

F

FOOT
cut two

E

F D D F

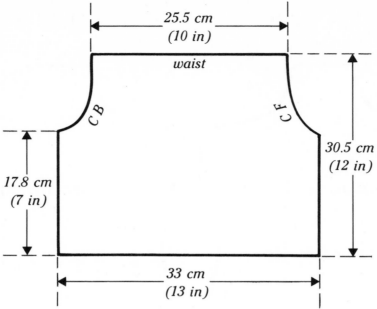

Figure 2.4

Measurements to make pattern for pantaloons.
CF = centre front   CB = centre back

91 cm (36 in) wide. The ties are made from a strip measuring 7.5 cm (3 in) by 91 cm (36 in).

Start by sewing bodice pieces together on the shoulders. Run a gathering thread around the head of each sleeve to ease in the fullness, then sew each sleeve in place to the bodice. Neaten wrist edges and trim with lace. Work an elastic row about 2.5 cm (1 in) above wrist, as you did for the legs of the pantaloons. Now close each underarm and bodice side in one continuous seam. Clip corner.

Gather long edge of skirt to fit waist and sew in place. Bring centre back edges to skirt together and sew from about 10 cm (4 in) below waist to lower edge. Make a hem and trim with lace. Neaten centre back opening of bodice and skirt and sew on snap fasteners. Finish neck edge with a self bias strip. Do remember to fit dress on body as you make it in order to determine just where the fastenings must be.

Finally make two ties by cutting the long strip in half so that you have two 45.5 cm (18 in) lengths. Make a narrow hem on all sides except one short end. Position this raw short end on the bodice front at the side, with hemmed long sides folded under to make the tie narrower. Now take a small tuck in bodice to lap over tie and hide the raw end. Top stitch with machine to hold tie in place. Fix remaining tie to other side of bodice then tie them together as a bow at the back.

Bonnet: A hank of raffia consists of a bundle of strands, each about 91 cm (36 in) long. Divide these into piles of thick and narrow strands then, using three strands at a time, start plaiting them together. Try to avoid having too many joins at the same place and occasionally use two thin strands in place of a thicker one. Make a plait several metres (yards) long and wind it into a ball to avoid tangling. When you feel that you have sufficient length, start coiling the plait around and sewing the coils in place to make a flat base. At this stage it is a good idea to look around for a mould that will fit the head of your cat and thus act as a former for the bonnet. It could be a margarine tub or small flower pot for instance.

Make the flat base to fit the bottom of the mould then continue sewing the plait to itself as you work up the sides of the mould and enclose it. When the required shape is achieved remove the mould and then perhaps add a brim by winding the plait backwards and forwards across the front of the bonnet. Decorate bonnet with artificial flowers and lace and finally sew on ribbon ties to come forward under the chin to make a bow.

CHAPTER THREE
Patchwork Pets

The piecing together of small fabric scraps offers many exciting challenges to felinophiles. Start with the pin cushion and pot holder which make clever use of cat prints, then make a portrait quilt or kit bag by sewing squares together. Traditionally cat names have been given to American nine-patch block patterns and examples of these have been used to make the cushions. Lastly Ancient Egyptian weaving techniques have provided the inspiration for a new form of string patchwork that is used to decorate the Duffle bag.

Log Cabin Pot Holder

LOG CABIN IS AMONGST THE MOST popular of all American patterns. It is the name given to a block built of strips around a central square. In this instance a cat print has been used for the central square and the strips are arranged in the variation known as Courthouse Steps.

Materials

23 cm (9 in) square of calico
23 cm (9 in) square of wadding
35.5 cm (14 in) by 28 cm (11 in) cotton print for backing
9 cm (3½ in) square of cat print fabric
six assorted plain and patterned prints for strips

Measurements

23 cm (9 in) square

To Make Up

Cut the six different fabrics into 4 cm (1½ in) wide strips. Arrange these around the central square to determine the best effect then cut two lengths of each fabric as follows:

Strip A	9 cm (3½ in)
B	14 cm (5¼ in)
C	14 cm (5¼ in)
D	19 cm (7½ in)
E	19 cm (7½ in)
F	23 cm (9 in)

Crease or mark diagonal lines with a pencil across the calico foundation square. Position the cat print centrally, right side up on the foundation square so that each corner touches a diagonal line, Figure 3.1. Sew cat print in place, 6 mm (¼ in) from the edge.

Starting with the upper side of the square, place a strip A right side down on the central square with edges together and sew in place. Turn strip upwards to bring right side into view and finger press it down. Now place remaining strip A against opposite lower edge of square and sew in place in the same way and again fold downwards, Figure 3.2. Now sew a strip B to each side and follow the sequence in Figure 3.3 so that the strips alternate in horizontal and vertical pairs.

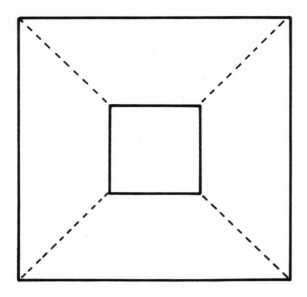

Figure 3.1

Foundation square showing central print in position with corners touching diagonal lines.

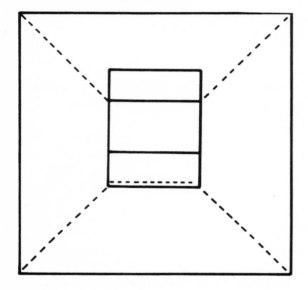

Figure 3.2

Foundation square showing first pair of strips in place. Lowermost strip is shown wrong side up, stitched in place, while uppermost strip is folded over right side up.

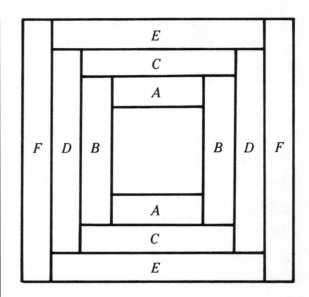

Figure 3.3

Completed block showing arrangement of strips in horizontal and vertical pairs.

Cut the backing fabric into a 28 cm (11 in) square. Lay this right side down on the worktable. Position wadding centrally on backing and in turn place log cabin block right side up on top of wadding. Trim tips off corners then fold 6 mm ($\frac{1}{4}$ in) forwards on all sides. Turn backing forwards again on to log cabin making an edge to the pot holder. Ladder stitch the mitred corners (Figure 3.6) and hem backing in place.

Make a strap from the remaining piece of backing material and sew it to the corner. A slightly quilted effect can be made by sewing through all thicknesses around the central square and just inside the edging strip.

Cathedral Window Pincushion

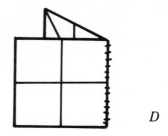

THIS UNUSUAL PINCUSHION IS A clever way of using small remnants of cat printed fabrics. The folds of the foundation square frame the cat print in a most attractive way to give the cathedral window effect.

Materials

two 23 cm (9 in) squares of plain coloured fabric for foundation squares
six 5 cm (2 in) squares of cat print for decorative squares
small amount of stuffing
matching thread

Measurements

10 cm (4 in) square

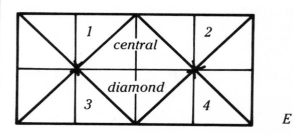

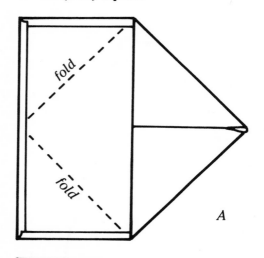

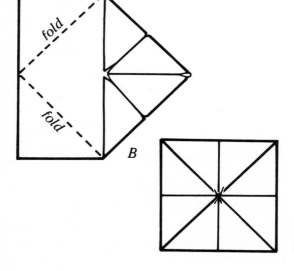

Figure 3.4

Cathedral Square. A. Foundation square showing raw edge turned in and two corners folded towards centre. B. Square turned over and folded as before. C. Centre points held with small cross stitch. D. Two foundation squares being sewn together. Place sides with tacked centres facing each other and oversew along one edge using smaller stitches. E. Squares opened out to show position of central diamond. F. Decorative square placed on central diamond showing two edges of foundation square rolled over and slip-stitched in place.

To Make Up

Using an iron, press a 6 mm ($\frac{1}{4}$ in) seam on all sides of both foundation squares. Find and mark centre of each square then with wrong side uppermost, fold in corners to meet at centre. Press to hold shape. Turn squares over, fold as before, iron edges and sew corners into position with a few small stitches as shown in Figure 3.4.

With right sides together, oversew the two foundation squares together along one side only. Cover the seam on the right side with a decorative square and pin in place. Roll over edges of foundation fabric into cat print and hem into place.

Place a decorative square on each half diamond space numbered 1 to 4 and sew in place by rolling foundation edges over as before. Fold excess cat print to wrong side and tack in place – do not cut off.

Before the sixth and last decorative square can be sewn in place the pin cushion must be folded in half, right sides together, and the two short sides sewn together to make a cylinder. Turn right side out and use the last decorative square to cover the seam.

Press cushion flat so that each side has a central diamond and four corner triangles of cat print. Oversew top edge, fill cushion with stuffing then neatly oversew bottom edge.

Dresden Plate Egg Cosies

FOUR PATCHES OF DRESDEN PLATE joined together and embroidered with a cat's face make a most unusual egg cosy. This can be further highlighted by carefully choosing prints to suggest specific cats.

Materials

Remnant of cotton print for cat patches
25 cm (10 in) × 15 cm (6 in) lining
25 cm (10 in) × 15 cm (6 in) wadding
15 cm (6 in) bias binding for tail
embroidery threads for features

Measurements

9 cm ($3\frac{1}{2}$ in) tall

To Make Up

Make a card template from pattern and cut four patches allowing a 6 mm ($\frac{1}{4}$ in) seam allowance. Join patches into a strip and press seams open. Using this shape as a pattern, cut a piece of wadding and pin to prepared patches. Cut away seam allowance from the wadding. Cut a lining the same size as the patches and with right sides together, sew round lower curved edges. Trim curves and clip corners.

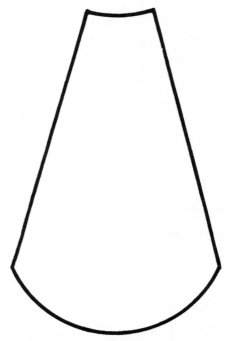

Pattern for templates (actual size)
add 6 mm ($\frac{1}{4}$ in) seam allowance

With right sides together sew side seam of patchwork only, then the lower edge of the lining. Turn cosy right side out. Work a row of running stitches along the bottom curved edge to keep lining to the wrong side. Turn under top outside edge only of cosy and oversew edges together with small stitches. Work a row of running stitches diagonally on each corner and slightly pull on thread to form the ears. More prominent ears can be made by taking a 4 cm (1½ in) square of fabric, folding it first in half diagonally then secondly into thirds. The resulting pointed ear with all raw edges at the base can then be placed in position on top of the head and caught in the seam. Embroider face. Keep the lining pulled away from the inside as you work on the cosy.

Fold bias binding in half lengthways and sew edges together to make the tail. Sew in place at back of cosy and knot the free end. Finally turn under raw edges of lining, sew together and push lining back inside cosy.

Catch Us If You Can Quilt

THIS PICTURE COT COVER OF A CAT looking longingly at the mice is a combination of machine pieced large and small squares, half-square triangles and hand appliquéd mice. The lightly quilted effect is achieved by working running stitches through all three layers of the cot cover.

Materials

91.5 cm (1 yd) cotton print for backing
91.5 cm (1 yd) wadding
91.5 cm (1 yd) dark blue for top
46 cm (18 in) of 91.5 cm (36 in) wide patterned blue for cat head
22.5 cm (9 in) of 91.5 cm (36 in) wide light blue
small amount of yellow and black fabric for eyes
dark blue quilting thread

Measurements

82 cm (32 in) by 62 cm (24½ in)

To Make Up

Make card templates from the patterns. Place large square template on dark blue and draw round square with yellow pencil, remembering to allow for a 6 mm (¼ in) seam allowance. Prepare and cut 34 dark blue squares in all. Draw round small square with suitable colouring pencil and after adding seam allowance cut 4 dark blue, 12 light blue and 18 patterned blue patches. Draw round half-square triangle and cut out, with seam allowance, 4 black, 4 yellow, 8 dark blue, 12 light blue and 16 patterned blue patches.

Assemble the cat's head first by sewing triangles together to make small squares, then four small squares to make a large square. Figure 3.5 shows the arrangement of fabrics needed to make each large square. Accurate seaming is needed if all squares are to fit together. Pin patches together by inserting pin through pencil line and checking that it emerges on the pencil line of the patch beneath. Only then will it be safe to sew patches together. Press seams open as you work. Complete the head by squaring the corners and filling the space between the ears with dark blue patches.

The top of the cover can now be made by framing the head with a single row of dark blue squares on all sides. An additional two rows

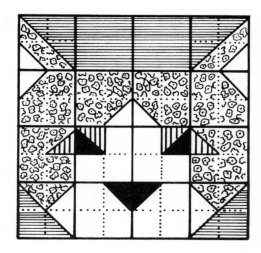

Figure 3.5

Diagram of cat's head showing arrangement of patches. Seaming of smaller squares and triangles making up each large square is indicated by dotted lines.

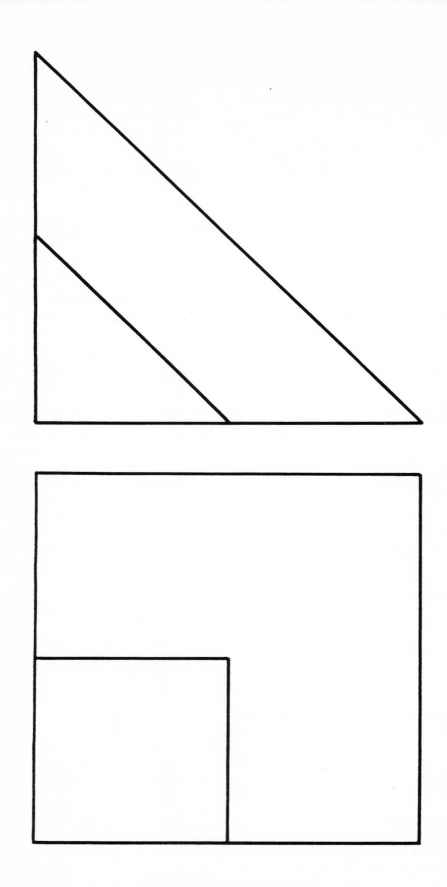

Pattern for template (actual size)
add 6 mm ($\frac{1}{4}$ in) seam allowance

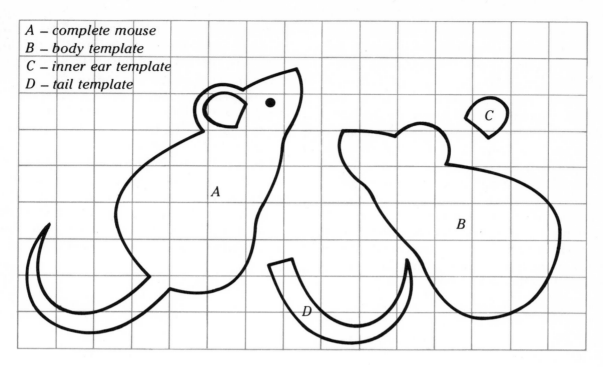

A – complete mouse
B – body template
C – inner ear template
D – tail template

Pattern grid. Catch us if you can quilt
one square=2.5 cm (1 in)

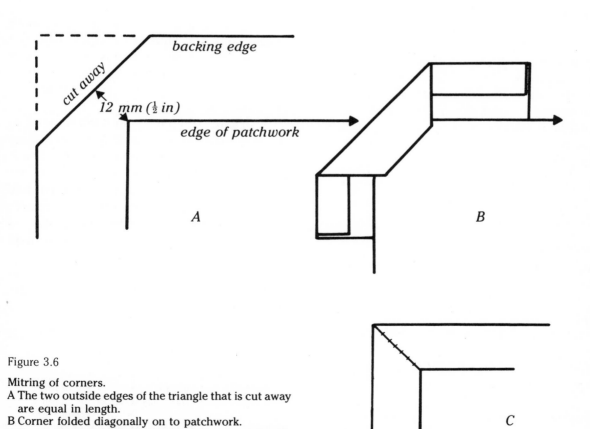

Figure 3.6

Mitring of corners.
A The two outside edges of the triangle that is cut away
  are equal in length.
B Corner folded diagonally on to patchwork.
C Hem turned on both sides and corner seam closed
  with ladder stitch.

beneath the head make the cover the required length for cot.

Prepare a full size pattern of the mouse, then cut stiff paper templates for the body, ear and tail of each mouse. Pin templates on the fabric and cut out each part with added seam allowance. Fold allowance over paper and gather, clipping where necessary to make corners and reduce bulk. Press completed parts under a damp cloth. Position mice on quilt and hem in place, removing templates as you work. Sew ear in place and embroider a small, black satin stitch eye.

Using the top as a guide, cut a piece of wadding the same size and the backing 4 cm ($1\frac{1}{2}$ in) larger all round. Lay backing right side down on table then place on this the wadding followed by the pieced top.

Mitre the corners, Figure 3.6, by cutting the corners off the backing, 12 mm ($\frac{1}{2}$ in) away from the patchwork, then fold backing on to patchwork and pin in place. Press a 12 mm ($\frac{1}{2}$ in) hem forward on all sides of backing, then turn all sides inwards on to the top and tack in place so that each corner forms a mitre. Close corners with ladder stitch and slip stitch edges in place. The backing makes a narrow border round the cot cover.

Use a quilting or bold stitch thread to work a row of small running stitches just inside the border. Pin or tack through the head and mice to hold all three layers together then work running stitch around the mice and the outside edge of head, nose and eyes of the cat.

Siamese Kit Bag

THIS SIAMESE HEAD HAS BEEN MADE by adapting the quilt cat. An additional row of small squares at the chin and the lowering of the eyes and nose alters the outline to give a foreign wedge-shaped head while the choice of colour determines the chocolate point. The squares are smaller than those used to make the quilt and are consequently handstitched over paper patches before being sewn together and appliquéd to the bag front.

Materials

23 cm (9 in) cream cotton
small amounts of chocolate, black and blue cotton
46 cm (18 in) of 114 cm (45 in) wide blue velvet
46 cm (18 in) of 114 cm (45 in) wide cotton print for lining
handles with 30.5 cm (12 in) slot and handgrip
stiff paper for patches

Measurements

51 cm (20 in) deep by 43 cm (17 in) wide

To Make Up

Make card templates for large and small squares and half square triangles from the patterns. Use these templates to cut upper patches as follows: 2 large squares, 8 large half square triangles, 20 small squares and 14 small half square triangles.

These same templates can then be used to cut fabric patches after making an allowance for seams. Cut fabric patches as follows: cream – 2 large squares, 16 small squares, 4 large half square triangles and 6 small half square triangles; chocolate – 4 small squares and 4 large half square triangles; black – 4 small half square triangles and blue – 4 small half square triangles.

Fold and tack fabric patches over paper patches. Take a needle threaded with white tacking cotton and, starting with a knot on the

Patchwork Pets (opposite)
Hanging up left to right: *Siamese kit bag, Cat's Cradle bag, Egyptian Cat roll bag, Log Cabin pot holders.*
In the centre left to right: *Cathedral Window pin cushion, Puss in the Corner cushion, Dresden Plate egg cosies, Puss in the Corner quilt, Cat's Cradle cushion.*
Bottom left: *Catch Us If You Can quilt.*

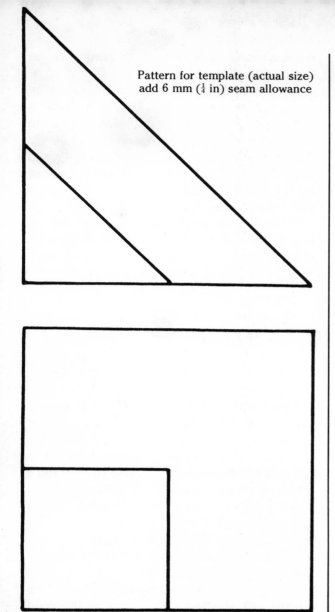

Pattern for template (actual size)
add 6 mm (¼ in) seam allowance

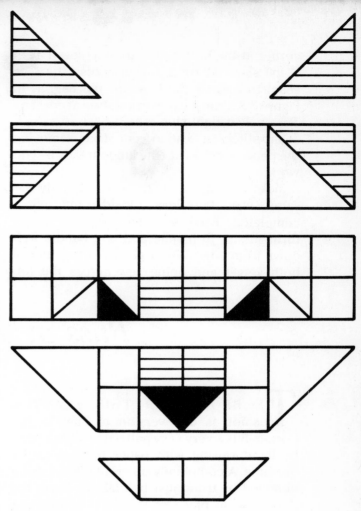

Figure 3.7

Siamese Kit Bag showing completed squares and
sections for each of the five strips.

right side, tack fabric to paper folding the
seam allowance closely over the paper and
taking particular care with the corners. Sew
half square triangles together first to make
squares, then follow Figure 3.7 to make five
strips which can in turn be joined to complete
the head.

With right sides together, fold the velvet in
half to make the bag. By keeping both selvedge
edges at the top the bag will have two side
seams. Sew up each side, from the fold, for
approximately 28 cm (11 in). Open out each

Cats to Quilt and Appliqué (opposite)
Left to right: *the Owl and the Pussycat apron, Just
Good Friends cushion, Sleepy Head cushion, Playful
Persians cushion, Daisy Chain quilt.*

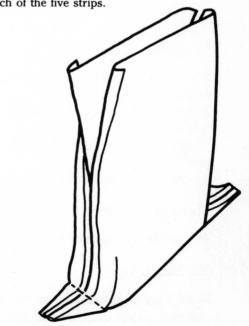

Figure 3.8

Bag showing formation of flat base by sewing at right
angles across the bottom of each side seam.

corner at the bottom in turn and sew a 5 cm (2 in) seam at right angles across the side seam to make a flat base for the bag, as in Figure 3.8. Trim away excess fabric at corners. Turn velvet right side out.

Slip stitch cat head to front of bag, removing the paper patches and tacking threads as you work.

Make a lining to fit the bag in exactly the same way but leave inside out when completed. Feed selvedge edge of velvet through slot in handle and pull handle well down from edge. With right sides together of both velvet and lining sew across the top remembering to fold in seam allowance on both sides.

Turn lining back into inside of bag and using a strong double thread, work a row of gathering stitches from side to side just 2.5 cm (1 in) down from the top. Pull handle up against stitching then pull gathering thread until bag fits slot. Work another row of gathering stitches beneath handle and again pull up until bag fits.

Attach remaining handle to other side of bag in the same way. Finally finish the bag by slip stitching the lining to the velvet on each side opening above the side seams.

Puss in the Corner

THE BLOCK FOR THIS SCATTER cushion is one version of Puss in the Corner. It is a very easy pattern to make either by hand sewing with paper patches or by machine. A completely different effect can be obtained by using just two fabrics – use the dark tone in place of the plain colour and substitute a light tone square in place of the plain colour square in each of the four corner units.

Materials

70 cm ($\frac{3}{4}$ yd) of 114 cm (45 in) wide light tone fabric
23 cm (9 in) of 114 cm (45 in) wide plain colour fabric
15 cm (6 in) of 114 cm (45 in) wide dark tone fabric
46 cm (18 in) square cushion pad

Measurements

46 cm (18 in) square cushion

To Make Up

Make card templates from the patterns and cut out paper patches as follows: 1 large square, 4 large rectangles, 4 small rectangles and 36 small squares.

Now pin the paper patches to wrong side of selected fabric making sure that they are on the straight grain. Leave a 6 mm ($\frac{1}{4}$ in) seam allowance all round each paper and cut out as follows: 16 small squares, 1 large square and 4 large rectangles from light tone fabric, 16 small squares from dark tone fabric and 4 small rectangles and 4 small squares from plain fabric. Lay all the patches out in order on a table so that you can check both the number cut and the colour selected.

Take a needle threaded with white tacking cotton and, starting with a knot on the right side, tack fabric to paper folding the seam allowance closely over the paper and taking particular care with the corners.

With matching thread which has been strengthened by pulling it over beeswax, sew patches together by placing two of them right sides together and oversewing the edge. Take very small stitches on the fold, avoiding the paper. Follow Figure 3.9 for assembly, which for a nine-square patch block is three rows of three squares. When the block is all sewn together, press it and carefully remove tacking stitches.

Cut a piece of light tone fabric for the back of the cushion and sew block to the backing leaving an opening on one side. Remove paper patches at this stage, insert cushion pad and then finish cushion by closing the gap.

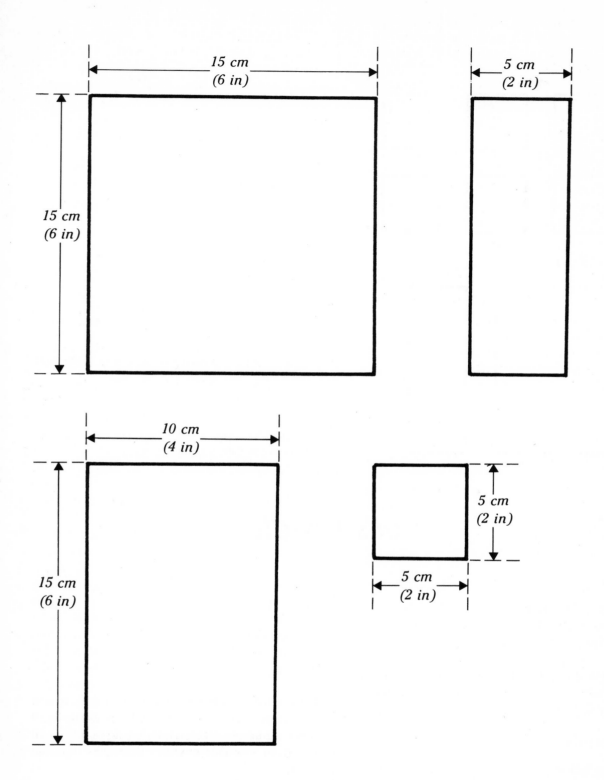

15 cm
(6 in)

15 cm
(6 in)

5 cm
(2 in)

10 cm
(4 in)

15 cm
(6 in)

5 cm
(2 in)

5 cm
(2 in)

Pattern for templates (with measurements)
add 6 mm ($\frac{1}{4}$ in) seam allowance

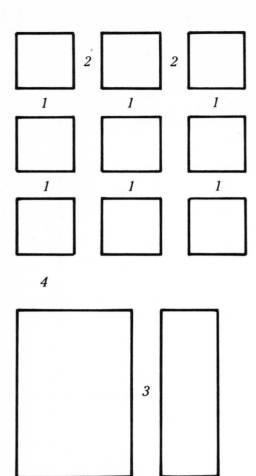

Figure 3.9

Puss in the Corner: showing sequence of joining patches
1 Sew small squares together to make three strips.
2 Sew strips to each other to make one large square. Make all other small nine-patch squares in the same way.
3 Sew two rectangles together to make a square. Complete similar squares.
4 Join nine-patch squares on top and bottom of square formed of two rectangles.
  Finish the block by making all three strips and joining as shown in Figure 3.11.

Cat's Cradle

THE BLOCK FOR THIS CUSHION IS A representation of the string game played by children. A loop of string is used to build interesting patterns which can be altered as the string is passed between pairs of hands. The starting position for many of the games is called Cat's Cradle.

Materials

Cotton fabrics 115 cm (45 in) wide in the following colours:
70 cm ($\frac{3}{4}$ yd) dark tone
30 cm (12 in) light tone
15 cm (6 in) contrast tone
38 cm (15 in) cushion pad

Measurements

38 cm (15 in) square cushion

To Make Up

Make card templates from pattern and cut out paper shapes as follows: 3 large squares, 6 small squares and 36 triangles. If you prefer to machine sew this cushion then you have no need to cut paper patches. Cut fabric patches with a 6 mm ($\frac{1}{4}$ in) seam allowance on all sides as follows: 1 large dark tone square, 2 large light tone squares, 6 small light tone squares, 18 dark tone triangles and finally 6 contrast coloured triangles.

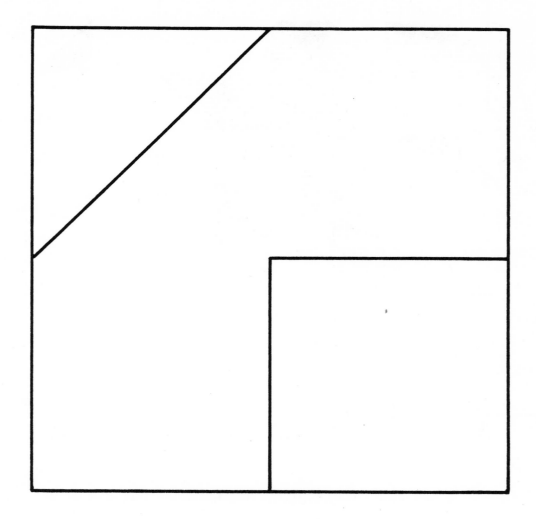

Pattern for templates (actual size)
add 6 mm (¼ in) seam allowance

Tack fabric over paper patches or machine fabric patches together along the pencilled seam line. Follow Figure 3.10 to assemble by sewing triangles in pairs to make small squares and then small squares together in pairs and so on working towards three rows of three squares and finally the completed block.

To make the frill, estimate the combined length of the four sides and cut a strip of dark tone fabric approximately three times as long. The width will be twice the finished width plus seam allowances. Join the short ends, then fold strip in half and run a gathering thread along the doubled cut edges. Draw up frill to fit exactly round the cushion. Cut a backing for the cushion then insert frill between block and backing, machine sew through all thicknesses. Leave an opening on one side, insert cushion pad and finally close opening.

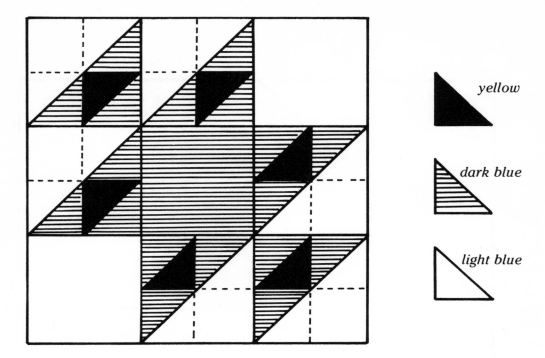

Figure 3.10

Cat's Cradle block showing arrangement of patches.
Broken line indicates seaming of smaller units within
larger squares.

yellow

dark blue

light blue

More American Block Patterns

A BLOCK IS A SQUARE OF FABRIC that has been made by sewing smaller pieces of fabric together. Some of the more popular patterns developed over the years have cat names such as Puss in the Corner and Cat's Cradle and instructions are given for making up both these blocks as cushion covers. Figure 3.11 shows yet more patterns and variations that you might like to try.

Similar blocks can be sewn together to make larger articles from placemats and tablecloths to bed covers. The attraction of making such a bed cover lies in the fact that all the blocks are first made separately which means that they are easy to handle. The colours used can be varied from block to block and patterned blocks can be separated by plain blocks thus allowing for even greater individuality.

On completion the blocks may be joined together so that they are parallel to the sides of the finished article or placed diagonally, giving a quite different effect. Furthermore they can be sewn to each other making an all-over design or they may be separated by strips of plain coloured fabric which forms a lattice work frame around the blocks.

The green and pink single bed cover illustrates many of the points already mentioned. The block pattern is another version of Puss in the Corner. The small corner squares use several different pink fabrics while the overall blocks have been set diagonally. The bed cover has then been hand quilted to highlight the units of the block.

Figure 3.11

Examples of nine-patch blocks all with names closely associated with cats. There are two variations of Puss in the Corner while Aunt Sukey's Choice is another name for Puss in Boots.

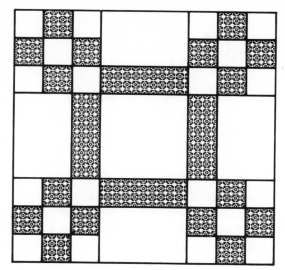

Puss in the corner (1)

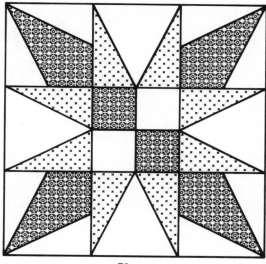

Claws

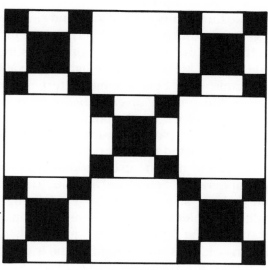

Puss in the corner (2)

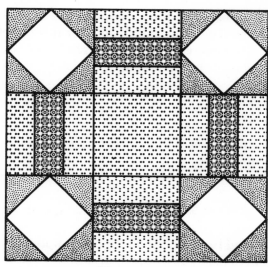

Kitty corner

Cat and Mice

Puss in Boots

Egyptian Cat

IT IS WIDELY BELIEVED THAT CATS were first domesticated by the Ancient Egyptians to hunt and retrieve ducks from amongst the reed beds of the Nile. They were also kept in vast numbers both as household pets and as temple animals. The latter were considered sacred to the goddess Bast, or Pasht, from which the word puss is said to be derived.

When family pets died they were mummified and buried in animal cemeteries. Some were bound with fabric strips whilst others had light and dark bandages interwoven to form various geometric patterns. The string patchwork for this duffel bag was inspired by the elaborate bandaging on one of the mummies in the British Museum.

Materials

114 cm (1¼ yd) of 91.5 cm (36 in) wide brown cotton
22.5 cm (9 in) of 91.5 cm (36 in) wide cream cotton
22.5 (9 in) of 91.5 cm (36 in) wide patterned print
40.5 cm (16 in) by 63.5 cm (25 in) wadding
15 cm (6 in) by 63.5 cm (25 in) iron-on Vilene
183 cm (2 yd) brown cord

Measurements

The bag is 53 cm (21 in) deep and has a circumference of 61 cm (24 in).

To Make Up

Prepare card templates from pattern pieces. A seam allowance is included in the templates.

Cut a lining of brown cotton measuring 63.5 cm (25 in) by 71 cm (28 in) and two circular base pieces each with a diameter of 21.5 cm (8½ in). Using templates A and B, cut 18 strips of each from the remaining brown fabric.

Cut 36 strips of cream cotton using template A. From the patterned print cut 4 strips measuring 63.5 cm (25 in) by 4 cm (1½ in), then use template A to cut a further 18 strips.

Make 18 units of string patchwork in the following way. Sew a cream strip to a patterned strip and a cream strip to a short brown strip. Now sew both pairs together by joining patterned strip to cream strip of second pair. Take nine of these units and sew a long brown strip across the top. For the remaining nine units, sew the long brown strip across the bottom. Figure 3.12 shows both units when completed.

Take three units of each kind and sew them together to make a band. Alternate the units so that the brown strips are continuous from side to side. Make two more bands in exactly the same way. Sew a long patterned strip across the bottom of each band, then join bands together and finish by sewing remaining long patterned strip across the top of the completed patchwork block.

Lay patchwork on top of wadding with right side uppermost. Sew round all sides to hold in place. Now sew a short edge of lining to patchwork block. Iron the Vilene to the inside of the lining close to the join with the patchwork. This will strengthen the top of the duffel bag and also reinforce the casing for the draw cord. Make a 3 cm (1¼ in) long buttonhole in the centre of the lining, approximately 7.5 cm (3 in) above the join with the patchwork. Figure 3.13 shows the position of the buttonhole. Now fold bag in half lengthways with right sides together and sew the side seam.

Make an opening in the seam for the second buttonhole. This will be level with the first buttonhole. These openings are for the draw cord. Turn bag tube right side out to neaten the buttonhole opening either by hand or machine zigzag. Now turn lining down on the inside leaving approximately 15 cm (6 in) on the outside above the patchwork. Sew both inner and outer lower edges together then turn bag inside out and sew double layer base in place. Turn bag right side out again and sew

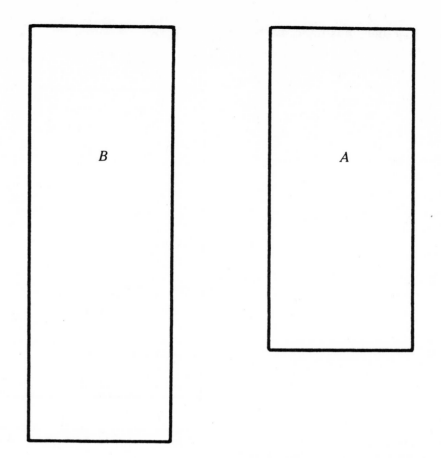

Patterns for templates (actual size)
seam allowance is included

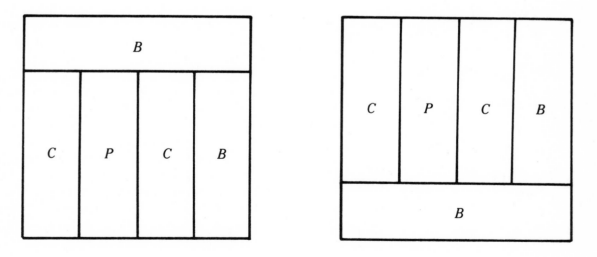

Figure 3.12

Completed units for Egyptian Cat patchwork.
C = cream   P = patterned print   B = brown

base and tube together making a narrow french seam on the outside.

Sew a channel for the draw cord enclosing the two openings through both thicknesses of the lining. Thread one end of cord into channel and encircle the bag twice before binding the ends of the cord securely together.

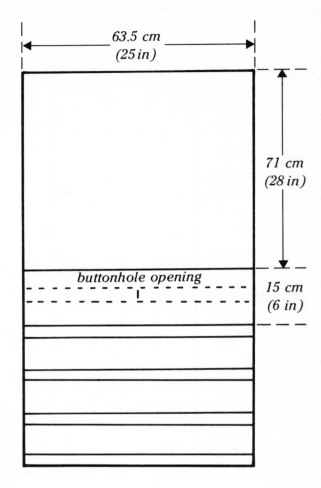

Figure 3.13

Diagram of bag and lining. Position of buttonhole opening is indicated in the draw cord channel marked by the broken line. This channel is worked after the side seam has been made and lining turned down inside bag.

CHAPTER FOUR

Cats to Quilt and Appliqué

Fabric motifs cut from one fabric and applied to another background fabric offer an effective way of both quickly and simply decorating household furnishings and clothes. These same motifs can be lightly padded, quilted or further decorated with embroidery stitches. The small cushions use different quilting techniques to produce low relief sculptured pictures.

Daisy Chain Quilt

SUNBONNET SUE IS AN EVER POPULAR American appliqué pattern for quilt tops and cushions. Here she is with her lucky black cat as the centre piece for a cot quilt. Together they are watching the butterflies. The picture is then surrounded by a daisy chain and framed on the outside by the border print. The daisy is called many different names by children throughout the British Isles but in Cumberland and Somerset it is known as Cat Posy.

Materials

A selection of small prints for the girl
Plain coloured cotton for butterflies, cat, hands and shoes
23 guipure daisies
90 cm (35½ in) by 71 cm (28 in) print for backing
69 cm (27¼ in) by 51 cm (20 in) plain fabric for quilt top
76 cm (30 in) by 57 cm (22½ in) wadding
pearl cotton for hand quilting
small pieces of wadding for butterflies and stuffing

Measurements

Quilt measures 56 cm (22 in) wide by 74 cm (29 in) long.

To Make Up

Enlarge the pattern for Sunbonnet Sue and cat. Cut out the various parts, except the bonnet crown, in stiff paper. The hatched line indicates extensions for hands, shoes and dress. Use these paper templates to cut out fabric pieces allowing a 6 mm (¼ in) turning on all edges. Turn under edges and tack folds in place.

Sew dress in place with slip stitch to the background top fabric, tucking in a hand and the shoes as you work around the dress. Apply pinafore overdress and sew on bow. Outline the ties of the bow with stem stitch. Complete the dress by sewing on sleeve and remaining hand.

There are two patterns for the bonnet crown. Use the larger shape to cut out the fabric. Turn under and tack the curved edge. Gather up the straight edge until the crown piece fits the smaller template which is in position on Sunbonnet Sue. Turn under the outer edges of the brim and tack. Sew brim in place and tuck in a piece of wadding to make it slightly padded. Sew crown in place, hemming outside edge first. Insert stuffing to pad hat then cover join between crown and brim with either a narrow band of fabric or a ribbon.

Prepare cat motif and sew in place.

Lay prepared top panel centrally on the layer of wadding. Tack both layers together. Hand quilt a running stitch round the outline of both Sue and the cat.

To make a butterfly, cut two 12.5 cm (5 in) squares of fabric and one of wadding. Draw the outline of the butterfly on one fabric square. Sandwich all three layers together with right sides out and wadding between. Work a row of machine straight stitch round the pencil outline. Alter machine to a wide but close zigzag stitch and work around wings, separating front and hind wings. Finish by working a wider zigzag down the centre of the body. Use small, sharp scissors to cut away excess fabric close to the stitching. Sew butterfly in place on quilt, taking stitches through body only, thus leaving wings free as if the butterfly is flying. Embroider antennae with stem stitch and finish with a french knot at the end. Make a second butterfly in the same way.

Cut guipure daisies into separate flowers. Arrange these in an oval around the appliquéd motifs. Sew each daisy in place through the petals with invisible stitches. Hand quilt with running stitch between the daisies to emphasize the oval.

Lay backing print right side down on table then lay top panel with wadding centrally on backing. The backing will extend 7.5 cm (3 in) beyond wadding on all sides. Cut off corners of backing then turn forward a 12 mm ($\frac{1}{2}$ in) hem around all sides. Turn edge forward again on to top panel. Mitre the corners (page 47) and slip stitch backing on to quilt surface. Finally, quilt all three layers together by working a row of running stitch round sides, 2 cm ($\frac{3}{4}$ in) in from the edge.

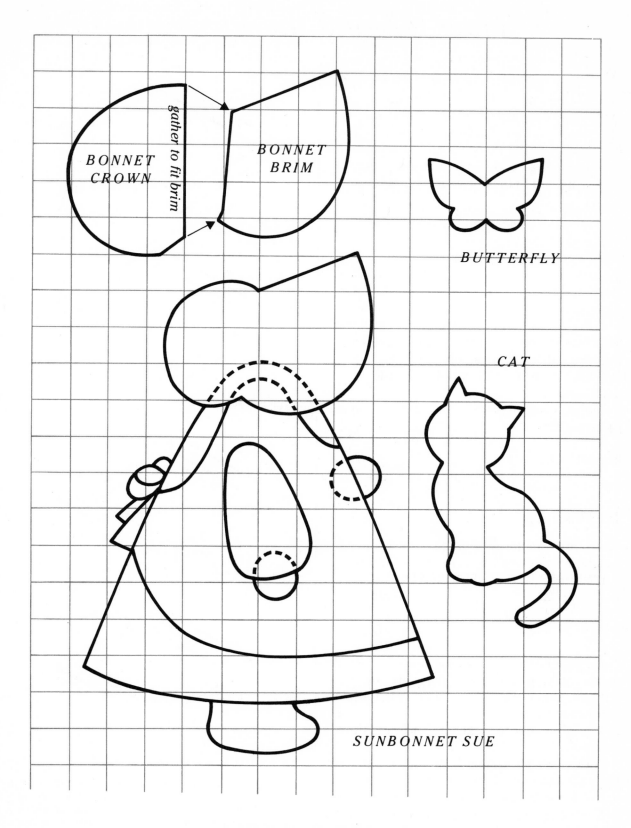

Pattern grid. **Daisy Chain quilt**
one square=2.5 cm (1 in)

The Owl and the Pussycat

HERE IS AN OPPORTUNITY TO combine different techniques and make an exciting fashion detail for an otherwise rather ordinary apron. The patchworked chain of owls and pussycats is appliquéd to a strip of plain fabric which in turn is applied to the apron as a border strip.

Materials

Selection of cotton prints for the patchwork
Guipure daisies for eyes of owls
30.5 cm (12 in) by 115 cm (45 in) wide plain cotton
Completed cotton print apron made to Vogue pattern 7256

Measurements

To fit an adult

To Make Up

Make card templates from the pattern and cut out paper patches for each unit as follows:

OWL		PUSSYCAT	
5B		1A	
2D		5B	
1E		3C	
		2D	
		1E	

Pin paper patches to wrong side of selected prints making sure that they are on the straight grain. Leave a 6 mm ($\frac{1}{4}$ in) seam allowance round each paper and cut out the required number to make four owls and three pussycats.

Fold seam allowance over paper patches and tack each one, Figure 4.1. Take particular care of the corners, especially for E. Sew patches together following the sequence BB, BBD and BDE to make 3 strips for the owl. Now sew the strips together to complete the unit.

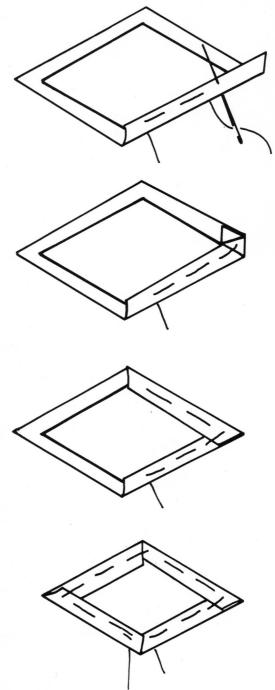

Figure 4.1

Working anti clockwise around the patch, fold fabric over paper. The sharp points at top and bottom of diamond have fabric folded three times while remaining two corners have fabric folded twice. Start with tacking thread knot on the right side. This will make it easier to remove all tacking threads at the end.

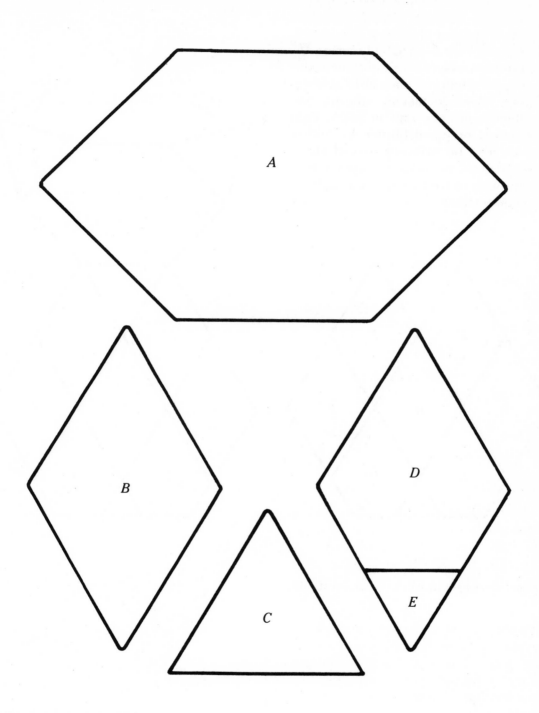

Patterns for templates (actual size)
add 6 mm ($\frac{1}{4}$ in) seam allowance

Make three more owls in the same way, Figure 4.2.

A similar sequence is followed to make the cat unit. Start by sewing CBB and then BBD and BDE, then sew strips together. Sew ears, C, to each side of A, then head to body across AC. Make two more pussycats in the same way.

Lay completed units on plain strip of fabric and arrange. Remove tacking stitches and papers, then hem each unit in place. Fold under edges of prepared border and either machine or hem on to lower part of apron skirt. Sew daisies on owls for eyes taking stitches through to back of apron to hold all three layers together.

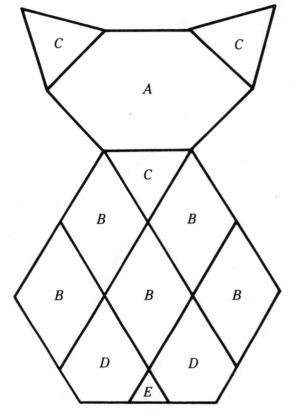

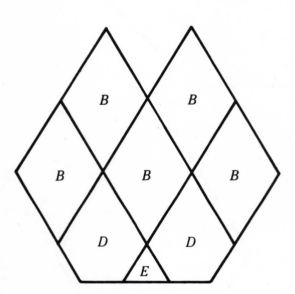

Figure 4.2

Arrangement of patches to make owl and pussycat units.

Cats to Embroider (opposite)
At the back: *gingham Dorothy bag, gingham cotton wool pouch, gingham Wet Ones cover.*
In the middle: *leopard box, jaguar box, gingham tissue box cover.*
At the front: *Cat in Clover.*

A Touch of Nostalgia

CREAM AND IVORY COLOURED satins, silks and georgettes with a hint of old lace have been used to make these sweet-smelling, softly quilted catnap pillows. The sixteenth century English herbalist William Turner described lavender as a "comfort to the brain". He advocated the use of lavender water to bathe the temples or to put fresh flowers in a quilted cap which could be worn on the head. Make these cushions to scatter on your bed for the same effect, filling them with sweet-smelling flowers from your garden.

Sleepy Head

Materials

two 30.5 cm (12 in) squares each of ivory coloured satin, wadding and muslin
a few handfuls of pot-pourri
Drima Bold Stitch in ivory
1 m (1 yd) of gathered lace

Measurements

25.5 cm (10 in) circular cushion

To Make Up

Enlarge the head and paws for the sleeping cat from the pattern grid. Transfer details to the right side of a square of satin. Make a sandwich of one square each of muslin, wadding and satin with right side facing uppermost. Tack all three layers together round the outside. Make a second sandwich in the same way using the three remaining squares.

Work the outline of the cat through all three layers in chain stitch with Drima Bold Stitch. The nose is worked with a triangular block of satin stitch while the whiskers are straight stitches. Enclose the worked area inside a 25.5 cm (10 in) circle of tacking stitches. Take tacking stitches through all three layers so that they show on the inside muslin layer.

Place both layers of cushion right sides together with muslin layers on the top and bottom. Sew around the edge using the tacking stitches as a guide to make the circle. Leave an opening. Trim edges and turn cushion right side out. Fill with a few handfuls of pot-pourri. Close opening. Sew gathered lace round the edge to finish the cushion.

Cats to Wind, Crochet and Knit (opposite)
At the back left to right: *grey kittens mittens, pompom puss belt, coiled cat basket.*
In the middle left to right: *black cats mittens, jungle paws mittens, Boots.*
At the front left to right: *Marmalade Moggy, playful kittens mittens, Boots' tabby companion.*

Just Good Friends

Materials

45 cm (18 in) any width satin
45 cm (18 in) each of wadding and muslin
2 large handfuls of lavender
Drima Bold Stitch, colour to match satin
61 cm (24 in) narrow cream ribbon for bows
61 cm (24 in) double edged ribbon
1.25 m (49 in) gathered lace

Measurements

Heart-shaped pillow approximately 30.5 cm
(12 in) wide by 33 cm (13 in) long.

To Make Up

Make a paper pattern for the heart-shape from
Figure 4.3. Cut this on folded paper in order to
get both sides of the heart. Use paper template
to cut two each of satin, wadding and muslin.

Enlarge drawing of cats from pattern grid.
Transfer outline detail to the right side of one
piece of satin. Lay this piece of satin on top of
a piece of wadding with layer of muslin
underneath. Tack all three layers together
around edge. Work outline of cats in chain
stitch with Drima Bold Stitch through all three
thicknesses. Whiskers are worked in straight
stitch.

Prepare the back of the cushion by
sandwiching together a piece of muslin
followed by wadding, then satin on top with
right side uppermost. Tack layers together
around the edge. Place front and back layers
of cushion together with satin surfaces facing.
Machine around edge leaving an opening for
turning. Trim edges, clip curves and turn right
side out.

Sew a length of double-sided ribbon down
each side of the cats. Fill cushion with some
lavender and close opening. Sew gathered
lace to edge of cushion and finish with a small
bow at the top of each length of ribbon.

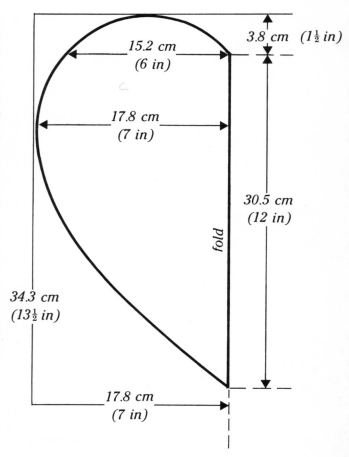

Figure 4.3

Measurements for heart-shaped pillow.

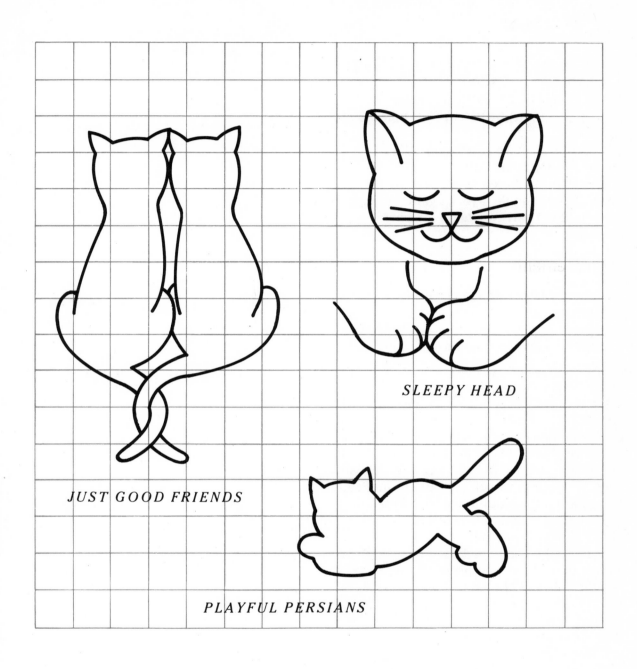

SLEEPY HEAD

JUST GOOD FRIENDS

PLAYFUL PERSIANS

Pattern grid. **A Touch of Nostalgia**
one square=2.5 cm (1 in)

Playful Persians

Materials

two 48 cm (19 in) by 23 cm (9 in) pieces of georgette
48 cm (19 in) by 23 cm (9 in) chiffon
two 48 cm (19 in) by 23 cm (9 in) pieces of wadding
23 cm (9 in) square rust coloured felt
cream Anchor Pearl Cotton
1.5 m (59 in) gathered lace
1.5 m (59 in) double layer of gathered lace
30 cm (12 in) narrow ribbon for bow
lavender

Measurements

Cushion measures 43 cm (17 in) by 17.5 cm (7 in).

To Make Up

Enlarge pattern grid to make a paper template of the Persian Kitten. Cut two from felt.

Lay one piece of georgette wrong side down on the table. Position felt kittens on top of georgette then cover with the piece of chiffon. A spot of glue will hold the kittens in place if necessary as pins would snag the delicate fabrics. Work a small backstitch in Pearl Cotton around the outline of each kitten thus sandwiching it between two layers of fabric. This is shadow quilting.

Position the completed front of cushion on a layer of wadding and baste all three layers together around the edge. Lay right side of second georgette piece to right side of cushion top and sew all together along two long sides and one short end. Trim corners and turn right side out. Cut second piece of wadding just a little smaller then insert into cushion. Scatter lavender between wadding layers and close cushion end.

Decorate the catnap pillow by first sewing the single layer of lace to the very edge then sew the double layer inside the edge. Make false mitres on the corners by careful folding to angle the turn. Position small bows as desired.

CHAPTER FIVE
Cats to Embroider

Make a picture with a difference by capturing the likeness of your family pet on canvas or learn how to distinguish between Leopards and Jaguars in a rather novel way by embroidering a pair of boxes. Whatever your choice you will find that all the articles have been designed with the minimum of basic stitches.

The Gingham Collection

THE SIMPLE CHARM OF CROSS STITCH cats on small gingham checks has been cleverly used to make a collection of co-ordinated accessories for nursery toiletries. Tissue boxes and Wet Ones have slip-over covers, cotton wool puffs a pouch, while a Dorothy Bag completes the collection. Select a darker thread to embroider the cats and then bias binding to match and broderie anglaise to trim.

Materials

1 m (39 in) of 114 cm (45 in) wide 5 mm check gingham
2 skeins six strand embroidery thread
4.5 m (5 yd) bias binding
30.5 cm (12 in) narrow elastic
2 m (2 yd) broderie anglaise
small piece of wadding for pouch
embroidery ring

Measurements

Pouch 20 cm (8 in) long
Dorothy Bag 18 cm (7 in) tall
Tissue Box cover 25 cm (10 in) long by 13 cm (5 in) wide
Wet Ones cover 16 cm (6½ in) tall

To Make Up

Precise measurements are given for making the pouch and Dorothy Bag but because tissue boxes are so variable in size you will need to take your own measurements and follow the general instructions. Slip-over covers for bottles and jars are made in exactly the same way as the cover for Wet Ones, bottles having an additional piece of elastic in the shoulder hem. Again take your own measurements and follow the general instructions for a good fit.

Several charts for cats are given in Figure 5.1, make your own selection or have a combination of all four. Each symbol on the charts represents one cross stitch, except the ears which are half cross stitch, and each stitch is worked over one 'square' of fabric. Work the embroidery in a frame so that fabric is kept taut and use only three strands of thread in needle throughout.

Work underneath stitches in one direction and cross all top stitches in the opposite direction making sure that crosses touch by inserting needle in same hole used for adjacent stitch. Avoid using knots by leaving an end on the back and working stitches over it and at the end, run the needle under four or five stitches on the back of the work. When embroidery is completed, steam press the fabric lightly on the wrong side.

Cover for Wet Ones

Cut gingham to fit round container adding 12 mm ($\frac{1}{2}$ in) to width for seam and 5 cm (2 in) to length for hems. Embroider four cats with upright tails leaving six squares between each cat. Sew on a length of bias binding just beneath the feet of the cats.

Fold gingham in half lengthways and with right sides facing sew edges together. Neaten the top edge with a narrow hem. Turn under bottom edge and hem, leaving an opening. Thread a length of narrow elastic through the bottom hem, pull up and fasten off. Don't pull elastic up too tight or container will not sit level. Close opening in hem. Gather a length of broderie anglaise to fit around the neck of the container. Turn under raw edge and sew in place with frill projecting upwards.

Dorothy Bag

Cut two pieces of gingham each measuring 30.5 cm (12 in) by 20 cm (8 in). Embroider four cats on one piece of gingham, 5 cm (2 in) up from bottom edge. Seam short sides of embroidered piece together. Press seam open flat. Gather a length of broderie anglaise and with raw edges level, baste it to the top edge of the bag.

Seam short sides of second gingham piece in same way. Press seam open. Place one tube inside the other with right sides facing. Sew together around top edge enclosing the gathered broderie anglaise. Turn bag right side out and baste together bottom edges of lining and bag.

Make two casings for the drawstring. These could be either of bias binding or gingham strips with edges turned in, and they need to be about 10 cm (5 in) long. Fold bag in half with seam at centre back. This locates the sides of the bags so that the casings can be sewn in place from side to side and about 2.5 cm (1 in) down from top edge. Use bias binding to make the drawstring. Take about 1 m (39 in), fold in half and machine edges together. Cut in half. Thread one length in

from side and completely around bag and out. Knot both ends together. Thread remaining length in from other side opening and again pass completely around bag. Finish by knotting the ends together.

For the base you will need to cut two 8 cm (3 in) squares of gingham. Treating the two squares as a single piece of double thickness, sew in place, clipping bag seam allowance to make neat corners. The bag is now ready for cotton wool pads, buds or whatever you like.

Cotton Wool Pouch

Cut two pieces of gingham and one of wadding each measuring 17.5 cm (7 in) by 26.5 cm (10$\frac{1}{2}$ in). Embroider cats in pairs at both short ends of one piece of gingham. Make sure that one pair is not upside down. Now make a sandwich of the wadding by placing a gingham piece on each side of wadding with right sides outermost. Baste three layers together around edges.

Neaten both short ends by covering with bias binding. Gather two equal lengths of broderie anglaise and with raw edges level, sew one strip down each long side of pouch. Overlap both ends of bias neatened sides to form a tube. Catch in place for about 6 mm ($\frac{1}{4}$ in).

Cut four gingham circles each with a diameter of 9 cm (3$\frac{1}{2}$ in) and likewise two circles of wadding. Make two three-layered pieces. These are the end wall gussets for the pouch. Sew one in place at each end of the pouch. Finish the pouch by making two bias binding bows and attach one at each side of the opening. Fill pouch with cotton wool puffs.

Tissue Box Cover

Choose a box with sufficient space either side of the opening to embroider the cats. Square tissue box covers should be made in the same way but would have cats embroidered on the sides rather than on the top.

Two rectangles of gingham need to be cut for the cover, one acting as a lining. To find the

Figure 5.1

Chart for cross stitch cats to work on gingham squares.

size of the rectangle you must measure the length, width and depth of your box carefully for a good fit. The long side of the rectangle will be the length of the box plus the depth twice and a further 4 cm (1¾ in) for hem. The short side of the rectangle will be the width of the box plus the depth twice and again 4 cm (1¾ in) for the hem.

Lay the box in position on the centre of one piece of gingham. Mark the area occupied by the top of the box with a tacking thread. Remove card covering to tissue box opening and use this as a template to mark the position of the opening on the gingham, Figure 5.2. You can now see the area where the cats are to be embroidered. When cats are finished lay this piece of gingham on the lining piece with right sides together and sew around the tacking line that marks the tissue box opening. Cut away opening area and clip seam allowance of the curve before turning lining and cover right side out. Press opening curve.

Lay cover over box and align openings. Do this with the embroidered surface facing the box and the lining outermost. Pin excess material together on each corner, remove cover and tack position of each corner seam. Sew seams, cut away excess material from corners. Make a narrow hem all around the base of the cover cutting away gingham if it is too bulky. Cover the hem with a length of bias binding and make a bow to cover the join. Alternatively you could make bows for all corners and even add a length of gathered broderie anglaise around the opening.

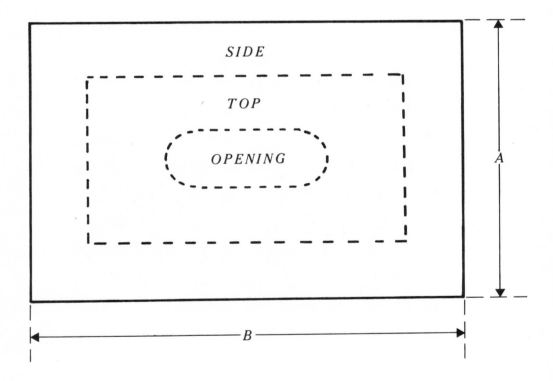

Figure 5.2

Cover for tissue box showing area occupied by sides, top and top opening.
A = side + width + side + double hem allowance
B = side + length + side + double hem allowance

A Pair of Boxes

FABRIC COVERED BOXES ARE VERY popular articles to make as they may be both decorative and practical at the same time. The tops and sides offer surfaces for embroidery while the insides can be tailor-made for the contents with compartments and trays as needed. The design for the tops of these boxes is based on the spots of jaguars and leopards. The spotted markings of these two big cats distinguish them from their near relatives, lions and tigers and also from one another. Since there is individual natural variation of spotting within a species as well as cross breeding between captive animals to produce such offspring as jagupards and lepuars it is little wonder that some are still confused.

In jaguars the black spots are arranged in rosettes of four or five with one or more central black spots, while leopards have rosettes with no spots enclosed in the centre. This difference in rosettes has been interpreted freely to make a design using no more than french knots and whipped spider's web.

Materials

1 m (39 in) dupion curtain fabric
1 m (39 in) Courtelle wadding
large sheet of thick grey card
large sheet of thinner card
three shades of embroidery thread to match dupion
small metallic beads
23 cm (9 in) square of felt
fabric glue
craft knife
cutting board
steel edge ruler
set square
fine sandpaper
strong thread for lacing

Measurements

Each box measures approximately 15 cm (6 in) by 10 cm (4 in) by 7.5 cm (3 in) deep.

To Make Up

Instructions are given for making a lined rectangular box with a single chamber. The lid sits on the sides and is held in place by a padded lining which fits down inside the box and so prevents it from sliding. In addition the lid is cut slightly larger than the box, the edge becoming a finger-hold for easy lifting.

To make a box successfully depends on several different factors which all relate to each other. Firstly the correct thickness of card must be used for the different parts of the box and it must be measured accurately and cut cleanly. The card is then padded and covered with fabric. The fabric is mitred at the corners and all edges are laced together to give a tight covering. Embroidery is worked before lacing and finally all covered card sections are ladder stitched together.

Many types of card are on sale in shops selling artists' material and as long as you remember to buy card that has enough rigidity for its purpose you will be alright. Mounting or backing board has been used for all the main parts while a thinner white card has been used for the lining where no weight is involved.

Use a sharp pencil to rule lines on the card and cut along this line with a craft knife held against a steel rule. With very thick card, the first cut will probably only score the surface. The knife can be placed in the track for the second cut and pressure applied to make a clean cut right through the card. A set square will help you to get accurate right angles which are necessary for without them the parts of the box will not fit together. The roughened edges of the card should be smoothed with fine sandpaper. Finally, as a precaution, label each piece of card as you cut it.

The most satisfactory way of glueing wadding or felt to card is to put a few spots of glue on the card, then to lay the card on a large piece of wadding or felt. When the glue is dry, the padding can be trimmed to shape. Be careful with the glue as too much can cause it to come through the wadding and spoil the feel. It might also make the wadding shrink.

When cutting the fabric to cover the card allow a generous turning all round, say 3.5 cm (1¼ in). The lid will need a little more as the edges will be exposed on the inside. Also watch where the grain of the fabric lies in relation to sections of the box. Some fabrics have variation in colour according to the way they lie while others may have an obvious weave on the weft. Dupion has a lighter wrong side and this has been used to make the lining of the box. There is sufficient material to make both boxes if sections are cut carefully side by side.

Mitred corners are the neatest way of covering corners as they are subsequently hidden within the making of the box. Fold fabric once, diagonally over a corner, then bring in each side in turn and pin in place, passing pins into the card. Ladder stitch the folded edges together with matching thread then move on to work the next corner. Bulldog clips and spring clothes pegs can be used to hold fabric in place if necessary but do be careful not to mark the fabric. Protect it with a piece of folded paper beneath the clip. Once the corners have been mitred the fabric can be laced in place using strong thread or thin crochet cotton. Lacing should be done evenly from side to side in both directions, Fig 5.3.

All boxes are made in sequence starting from the base. Since the thickness of padding and fabric covering must be taken into consideration it makes good sense to finish each stage before measuring and cutting for the next. Keep in mind that boxmaking is a slow and precise craft. Cut a base for your box from thick card measuring 15 cm (6 in) by 10 cm (4 in). Glue on padding of felt then cover with fabric, mitre the corners and lace in place.

Use covered base to take measurements for the sides. The long sides should equal the length of the base plus two thicknesses for the short ends and Fig 5.3 shows how to achieve this. Use scrap pieces of card laid against base to help take measurements and remember to allow a little for the thickness of the covering. Sides are cut from thick card and the height is 6 cm (2½ in).

Pad side pieces of box with wadding. The size of the fabric covering is equal to the total length of the four sides plus turnings all round. Lay one padded long side on the fabric and pin in position to hold it in place. Mitre the two corners then begin to lace across the card from top to bottom. Push a short side up close to the long side, pin in place to hold firm, then lace. Continue with second long side and finally second short side and finish by making both mitres on other corners.

Now bend sides into a rectangle, with lacing on the inside, making sure that short sides lie inside long sides to give a good fit and pleasing appearance to your box. Ladder stitch the ends together to make a nearly invisible join. Push finished side walls over the base and pin in place. Ladder stitch base to sides. Sometimes a curved needle will be found useful at this point.

The lining is essentially another box cut from thin card and placed inside with the padding also on the inside. Remember to use the reverse side of the dupion for the lining. Make the base first. Measure the inside box length and width and remember to cut slightly smaller to take into account the thickness of the fabric covering. Pad and lace inside lining base as box base. When finished, place in box in position.

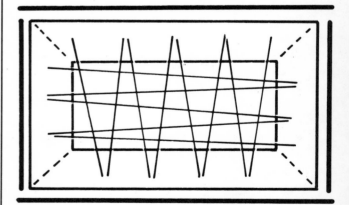

Figure 5.3

Base of box with fabric covering laced in place and corners mitred. The sides of the box show how the long sides overlap the short ends.

Take measurements for side linings as for box sides with long sides butting over short sides and short sides being width of box less two thicknesses of card. The height should be cut level width the box sides. Cut card and pad. Cut fabric, then pin all pieces together and put lining inside box to check that all fits. Finish in exactly the same way as for the box. Oversew lining base to lining sides and again put into box to check fit. You can either put glue on the inside base to hold the lining in place or ladder stitch lining sides to box sides around the top edge.

A further decorative effect can be achieved by inserting a narrow velvet ribbon all around the edge between the lining and box. This would act as a fillet of colour providing more interest to the inside. Likewise it could act as a filler if the lining had been cut too small.

Now that the main part of the box is finished you can take the measurements for the lid. Add a few millimetres on each side so that the lid projects just over the edge of the box. Cut lid from thick card and pad in the usual way. Tack outline of lid on a piece of dupion and mount this in a frame ready for the embroidery.

Figure 5.4 shows the rosettes of jaguars and leopards. Using these as a guide draw them free hand on a piece of thin paper and make them slightly larger at the same time. Working on one rosette at a time, cut around each spot and arrange the paper templates on the design area. Move them around until you are pleased with the appearance, then pin them in place. Because the rosette of the leopard is smaller, two of the spots have been re-used on the side to make it appear as if another rosette is there.

JAGUAR   *LEOPARD*

Figure 5.4

Diagram of rosettes from jaguars and leopards.

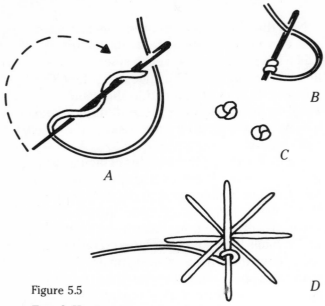

Figure 5.5

French Knots

A. Bring thread through fabric and wrap twice around needle. Pull up on thread to draw coils around needle then swing needle back to where thread starts.

B. Insert needle beside thread and pull down through coil to form a surface knot.

Whipped Spider's Web

C. Work a grid of long straight stitches. Bring thread out near centre and pass over and under spoke immediately behind. Pass forward under next spoke, working clockwise, then repeat whipping. Continue in this way working around the grid until all the spokes are covered.

Following Figure 5.5 work a few light coloured french knots around the edge of each piece of paper then the paper can be removed. Work between 3 and 5 whipped spider's web stitches in dark thread in the centre of each spot. Fill in remainder of spot area with medium colour french knots. Scatter a few metallic beads amongst the knots and catch stitch in place. The fabric can now be laced in place on the lid. Since about 1.5 cm (½ in) of the underside of the lid will be seen you will need to cut larger turnings and work very careful mitres on each corner.

The lid lining holds the lid in place and needs to be an exact fit. Measure the inside opening of the box, remembering to deduct for the thickness of fabric and cut a thick card. Pad in the usual way. Cut a fabric covering and lace this in place with the wrong side of the fabric showing. The two sections of the lid can now either be ladder stitched or glued together.

Having constructed this pair of boxes you may well be challenged into designing your own and being more ambitious with rising linings and flush lids. They are certainly very rewarding articles to make and always prove popular as presents.

Cat in Clover

ACAPTURED LIKENESS WORKED ON canvas with fabric and lace trim surround makes a focal point for a most unusual but distinctive slip-on cover that fits the standard A4 ring bind folder. Use it to hold mementoes of cat shows, photographs, recipes or magazines. Although work of this nature is more frequently framed behind glass, a cover is permanent enough to give pleasure for as long as it is treated with respect. You may even like to capture the likeness of your own family pet instead of copying the silver grey tabby and thus make a more personalised article.

Measurements

25 cm (10 in) by 32 cm (12½ in)

Materials

25 cm (10 in) square of mono canvas with 18 threads to the inch
square or rectangular embroidery frame
white and two shades of grey Anchor tapisserie wool for cat
white, black, pink and gold six strand embroidery thread for cat
three shades of pink background wool for background
cream embroidery thread for surround
71 cm (28 in) of 114 cm (45 in) wide pink furnishing cotton
1 m (1 yd) each of assorted ribbons and lace for surround
A4 ring bind folder

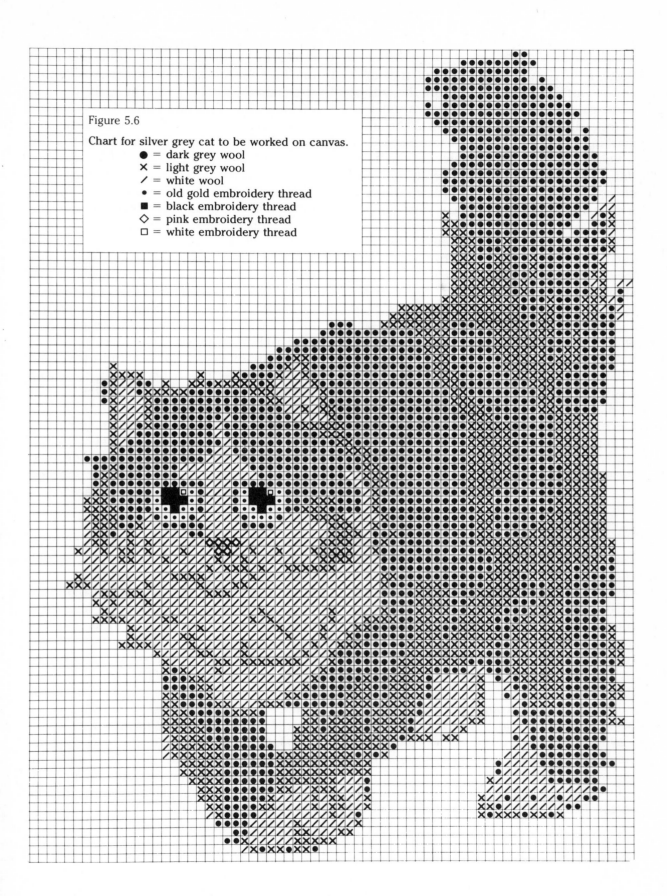

Figure 5.6

Chart for silver grey cat to be worked on canvas.
● = dark grey wool
✕ = light grey wool
╱ = white wool
• = old gold embroidery thread
■ = black embroidery thread
◇ = pink embroidery thread
□ = white embroidery thread

To Make Up

Prepare the canvas first by binding the edges and mounting on the frame. Work the outline of the cat carefully and also the eyes and nose by following Figure 5.6, then fill in all the tabby markings. The cat is worked in tapisserie wool which is really a little too thick for the holes but does give a desirable, slightly textured effect. Work with small lengths of wool in your needle, thus avoiding undue wear on the thread.

Tent stitch is used throughout for both the cat and background. Work backwards and forwards making sure that all the stitches slope in the same direction and that they are longer on the reverse side, Figure 5.7. Start each new thread with a knot on the right side which may be cut off later and finish each thread by weaving in the end.

For those who wish to work a picture of their own cat on canvas it will be necessary to work from a colour transparency. Tape a piece of white paper, the size of your canvas, to your wall then project the slide on to the paper. It is now a simple matter to draw round the outline and map out the areas of colouring in your cat. Transfer all detail to the canvas and complete embroidery in tent stitch as already outlined.

The background is worked with a thinner 2 ply background wool in three shades of pink which include a rich plum tone. Surround the cat with a bright clover pink, then work a narrow border, say two rows of plum, all round this. Invert the corners for added interest. Finally, work an outer band of the remaining pink colour. The finished size should measure 14.5 cm ($5\frac{3}{4}$ in) by 17 cm ($6\frac{3}{4}$ in).

Remove canvas from frame and stretch it back to shape. Trim excess canvas away leaving a border of three threads on all four sides. The canvas is now ready to sew on to the front of the cover.

Cut the selvedge edges away from the cotton fabric, then trim it to 104 cm (41 in) wide. Cut fabric in half across the width so that you have two similar sized pieces, 35.5 cm (14 in) by 71 cm (28 in), one for the cover and one for a self lining. Using one piece only, fold it around the folder to determine the position of flaps, front, back and spine. The area of the front cover can be outlined with a tacking thread. Remember to allow a seam margin on all outside edges, Figure 5.8.

Position the canvas-work panel centrally on the front and tack in place. Use all six strands of cream coloured embroidery thread and work satin stitches over the three threads left on the edge of the canvas.

The canvas panel can be left as it is or framed further as you wish. This will rather depend on the type of fabric that you are using for the cover. The photographed example has an outer frame of gently gathered pink lace with ribbon insertion. First there is a wide cream ribbon to pick up the satin stitches and then a narrower plum ribbon on top to pick up the plum tent stitch border in the canvas panel.

Prepare sufficient lace with ribbon already in place to reach round the panel and allow extra to mitre the corners. Carefully position lace and sew in place with invisible stitches, folding corners to give the appearance of mitres.

Place right side of cover to right side of lining and sew both pieces together round all edges leaving a 15 cm (6 in) opening on one short side. Trim excess fabric away and cut off corners to reduce bulk. Turn cover right side out and close opening. Press cover now if it is creased, being careful not to flatten the canvas and lace.

Wrap cover over folder to check size before finally sewing together. The fit must be snug with no wrinkles and yet not so tight that it could be damaged when removing. When satisfied with the fit, put pins in to mark where top and bottom edges of inside flaps meet the outside cover. Remove cover from folder by opening back the folder and sliding out. Ladder stitch flaps in place securely, then fit cover back on to folder.

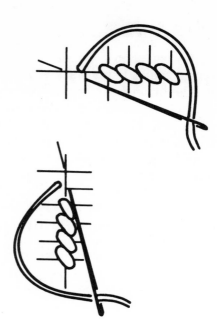

Figure 5.7

Tent stitch worked both vertically and horizontally.

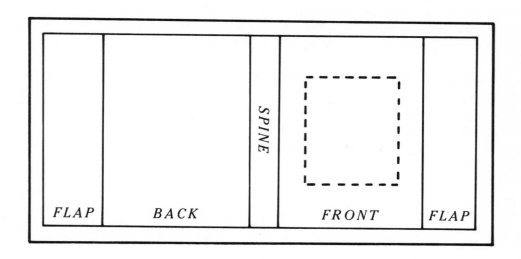

Figure 5.8

Top layer of cover showing front and back areas marked out, as well as the outline for the front panel and a generous outer seam allowance.

Cats to Wind, Crochet and Knit

Modern yarns whether wiry, soft, coarse or light offer an overwhelming variety of textures to work with while the colours have the added attraction of being pure, randomly dyed or even variegated by the combination of different strands. Be adventurous with your selection even though the patterns have been designed with a specific texture and colour and the quantity calculated accordingly.

Pompom Puss

THE OLD FASHIONED BUT STILL popular cut woolly ball which is made by winding wool on a circular cardboard foundation has provided the inspiration for this novelty belt. However, instead of using separate templates to make the head and body, the two have been combined to make a single template with protective flanges at each end. These flanges prevent the wool from slipping off the ends while the centre slit is used to pass the binding thread round the wool winding.

Materials

two 20 g balls of black 4 ply wool
4 green wooden beads
7.5 cm (3 in) square black felt
15 cm (6 in) square stiff card
strong black thread

Measurements

length of belt is 143 cm (56 in)
length of cat including tail is 16 cm (6¼ in)

To Make Up

Cut two cardboard templates from the full size pattern, using a craft knife if necessary to cut the central slit.

Wind a double layer of wool along the card template by using wool from both balls at the same time. The winding must be even and done loosely throughout. Starting at one end of the slit and winding over the card to the other end should require 25 winds and thus complete a single wrap. Continue winding by working backwards and forwards until eight wraps in all have been completed.

Pass a long double length of strong thread around the wrappings, by taking the threads through the slits at each end. Tie ends together and repeat the binding for a second time. The threads lying along each side can now be sewn together securely by threading the loose ends into a needle and stitching to and fro through the central slit, Figure 6.1.

Cut nine lengths of wool, each measuring 30.5 cm (12 in). Fold these in half and stitch the midway point to the bottom of the cat. Divide strands into three bunches and plait for

Pattern for cardboard foundation (actual size)

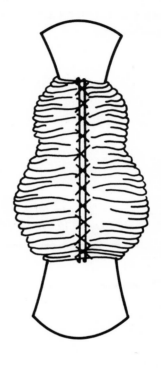

Figure 6.1

Diagram of wool wrapped around frame and central binding threads stitched in place, crossways, from side to side through central slit.

required length. Fasten off end of plait and trim the loose ends.

The wool can now be cut at the edges with either scissors or knife. Cut a few layers at a time until all the underneath layers are finally free. Ease cut wool away from the template. Make a second Pompom Puss in the same way, using the second template.

The belt is made from 21 strands cut at 140 cm (55 in). Fasten all strands together 7.5 cm (3 in) from one end and then proceed

to make a plait. Finish the plait 7.5 cm (3 in) from the other end and fasten off. Bind loose ends by closely wrapping wool down the ends making a coil. Sew end of coil to head of cat. Finish the other end of the belt in the same way.

Cut felt ear shapes and sew in place, then sew beads in position as eyes. Finally, trim any uneven lengths of wool on the body so that a good outline is obtained.

Boots

BOOTS AND HIS TABBY COMPANION are cut wool cats with a difference. They have a wire skeleton as part of their binding and this enables them to be bent into various positions. Also, unlike the cut wool Pompom Puss which is made on a cardboard frame, these cats are wound on an adjustable hairpin crochet Quadframe.

Materials

40 g ball (163 m – 178 yd) black mohair wool
small ball white mohair wool
82 cm (32½ in) thin plastic-covered garden wire
2 green glass buttons with shanks
black model paint
strong carpet thread
wire cutters and snipe-nosed pliers
Quadframe
embroidery thread for nose

Measurements

10 cm (4 in) tall and 17.5 cm (7 in) long

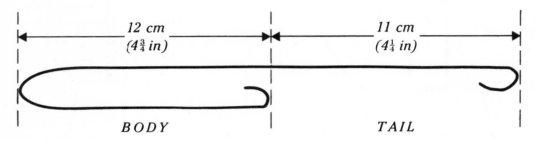

Figure 6.2

Shaping of wire to make double body section and single tail section. Each end is turned back into a small loop.

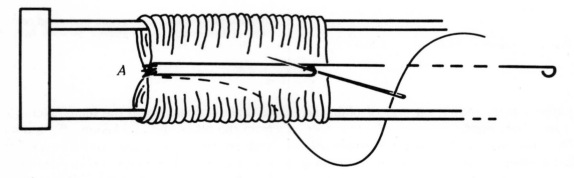

Figure 6.3

Wool is bound to the body wire section by oversewing the front end of the wrapping to the wire at A. The binding thread is then passed along the underside and brought up to the top by passing the needle through the small loop at the end of the body section and overcasting as at the front.

To Make Up

Set the Quadframe over six holes. This is done by positioning a rod in a hole and placing the second rod five holes away. Clamp the bridge over the free ends of the rods to keep them in place. Now wind wool evenly over the rods working backwards and forwards for a distance of 14 cm (5½ in) and making 450 winds in all.

Cut a length of wire 36 cm (14½ in) and bend into shape, Figure 6.2. Each end is turned back over the pliers to make a small loop. Lay doubled end of wire centrally over wool on Quadframe. Using strong double thread, overcast end of wool layers to bend in the wire, Figure 6.3. When the wire is securely attached to the wool take a long stitch down the back and bring the needle up beyond the layers so that all the wool is caught in the stitch. Now pass needle through small loop and pull up tightly so that wool fits the length of wire and again overcast the end securely.

The wire can now be fastened to the long thread on the back by passing the needle to and fro over the wire on top and the long thread beneath as each stitch is taken. Pull up tightly as you work the overcasting. This must be very secure if the cat is not to unravel. Remove the body from the frame.

Reset the rods over four holes to make the tail. Wind black wool 250 times over the frame for a distance of 11 cm (4¼ in). Place completed body section at one end of tail so that the protruding single length of wire lies centrally along tail winding. Overcast each end in turn, the body loop being used for the base of the tail. Remember to take long stitch down back of tail then bind wire to thread and when finished remove completed body/tail from Quadframe.

The body needs additional thickening for the head and this is achieved by winding a separate head and chin pad both of which are bound with strong thread only.

To make the head pad, set the frame over six holes and wind 100 wraps of black wool over a distance of 5 cm (2 in). Bind the wool with thread and catch top and bottom long stitches together by sewing securely through the layers and pulling up tightly. Remove from the frame.

The chin pad consists of 50 wraps of white wool wound on frame for a distance of 3 cm (1¼ in) with rods set over four holes. Bind layers together with thread and remove from frame.

The legs are made in pairs with the rods set over four holes. Wind on 50 wraps of white wool followed by 200 wraps of black and 50 more of white for a length of 11 cm (4¼ in). Cut wire 22 cm (8½ in) long and bend as shown in Figure 6.4. Position wire centrally and overcast wool to loops and bind layers closely together by following instructions for body. Remove from frame and make a second pair of legs in the same way.

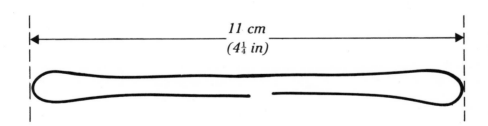

11 cm
(4¼ in)

Figure 6.4

Shape of wire for making a pair of legs. This ensures that the ends of the wires are safely in the middle of the section where they can be bound to the wool and covered.

All the sections of the cat have now been prepared and are ready to be assembled. The legs are joined to the body first. Hold wire side of both body and hind legs facing towards you. Place hind legs across body and cross stitch the legs centrally to the body, working the stitches over both wires. Tie off ends securely. Again holding wire side facing towards you, sew front legs to body in same way.

After the legs have been positioned, sew head and chin pads to upper and lower sides of head respectively. Make sure that both leading edges are level with the front edge of the body, Figure 6.5. Close wire loops where possible with the pliers, then cut all the wool loops with scissors.

To make Boots stand, his legs must be bent downwards and the tips of the feet turned forwards. Holding him in your left hand, with thumb between forelegs and resting on chest, bend his head up and forwards, Figure 6.6. Leave the tail horizontal until it has been trimmed, then bend into required position.

Shaping and trimming the wool to sculpture the cat is the most rewarding part of cut wool toy making. You should do it slowly, turning your animal from side to side as you work. It is also advisable to have some pictures of cats nearby to guide you, especially when trimming the head. At all times, be careful not to cut into overcasting stitches on the ends of the wires.

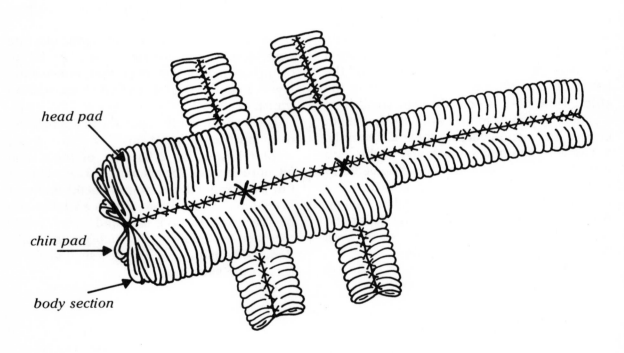

head pad

chin pad

body section

Figure 6.5

Boots showing all sections securely sewn together, from the top side. The extra large cross stitches mark the position where the legs are joined to the body.

Start by rounding off the back of the body at the base of the tail then clip tail to a tapered tip. Trim legs and clip shaped feet. Very little shaping is needed for the legs, it is really the bulk that is being reduced. Clip any long wool off the back, working towards the neck with the point of your scissors. Now trim the chest with the scissors again working towards the neck. Trim around the neck so that the head is separated from the body.

The head requires more skill in shaping so work slowly, always checking appearance. Cut from the nose upwards to flatten the face, then carefully shape the head, being careful not to reduce the width of the face by cutting too much off the cheeks. Clip up forehead to lower head between ears, then working very slowly raise the ears from the nap by cutting little bits at a time. If you find this too difficult, stitch felt ears in place.

Paint pupils on the buttons and when completely dry, sew them in place. Finally, embroider a few satin stitches for the nose.

The Tabby cat is made to the same measurements but with a smaller ball of variegated wool. Consequently more white is needed to make up the difference and to give the necessary shape and bulk. Two bodies are made, the upper tabby being overcast to the wire frame while the lower white section is bound with thread then stitched to the upper layer in the same way as the chin pad was joined on to the head. The eyes are black beads.

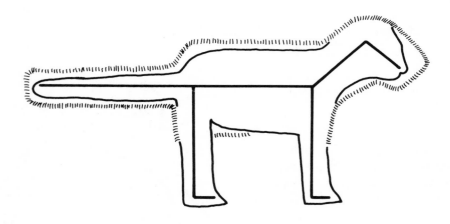

Figure 6.6

Boots, bent into position ready for sculpturing, the tail is left horizontal until clipping is completed. Broken line indicates original thickness that must be trimmed away to obtain outline of continuous line profile.

Coiled Cat

COILING, A BASIC TECHNIQUE FOR basketry, is also suited to constructing three-dimensional forms. In this instance the core is a length of clothesline while the weft is a grey and white bouclé wool yarn. As the core is wrapped with the wool, it is shaped into coils which in turn are stitched together and built into the required form.

Materials

9.15 m (10 yd) rope clothesline
three 50 g balls Sirdar Sheba wool
2 green or yellow wooden beads
small ball white mohair wool
4.00 mm crochet hook
few yards of black wool
embroidery thread for nose
nylon fishing line for whiskers

Measurements

15 cm (6 in) tall

To Make Up

Lid: Cut a 1.85 m (2 yd) length of clothesline for the core and taper one end with a sharp knife. Now cut a 60 cm (2 ft) length of yarn and lay the yarn end against the tapered core. Wind the yarn towards the tapered end, covering the loose end of yarn in the process. Start the coiling by folding the wrapped end of the core and winding more yarn around both pieces of core. Continue bending core into circular coil and stitch to hold in place. Use Lazy Squaw stitch to hold first few coils in place, Figure 6.7. Hold the yarn behind the top coil and pass it over both top and lower coils to bring it out behind the coils ready to wrap it round the top coil a few more times before working the next Lazy Squaw stitch.

Work three complete coils after the centre has been started. Coils are easiest formed in a clockwise direction when working the lid. The eyes are incorporated in the coiling but need to have pupils made first. Do this by winding a

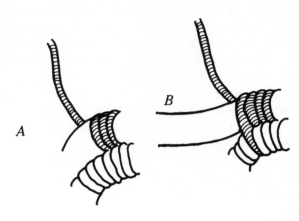

Figure 6.7

The Lazy Squaw Stitch. In A, the yarn is behind the upper coil ready to stitch over both upper and lower coils on the front. B shows the yarn passed under the lower coil to the back and brought up to the top again. Wind yarn around the top coil only a few more times before working another Lazy Squaw Stitch. Working yarn is shown shaded for clarity.

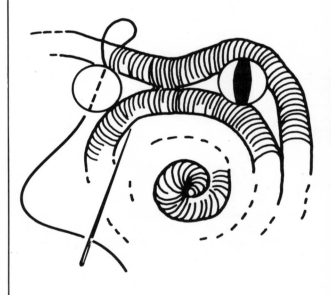

Figure 6.8

Coiling of lid, showing how the beads are inserted in position to make the eyes.

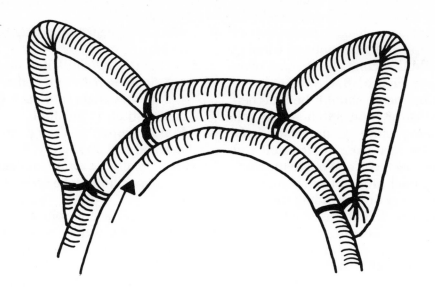

Figure 6.9

Construction of ears by bending of coil. The base of the ears are held in place by stitches as indicated and arrows show direction of coiling.

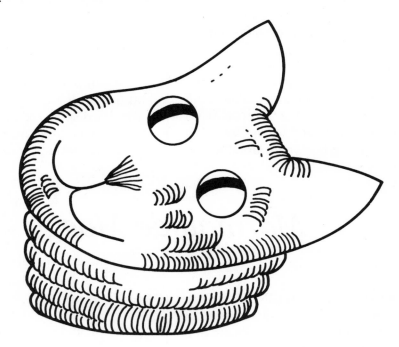

Figure 6.10

Construction of lid with collar showing how the tapered end is wound into last coil and finished off.

few layers of black wool through the bead and tie off at the back leaving the ends hanging. Now thread eye on to weft yarn and bring needle under bottom coil, back through bead and wind over top coil and continue winding and coiling until second bead has been stitched in place, Figure 6.8.

The coils, by now, should be stitched together with figure eight stitch which will make the coiling more secure than Lazy Squaw. Bring the yarn over the top coil and then behind the lower coil and out to the front and finally over the lower coil and behind the top coil ready to continue winding the core. Work one complete coil at this stage.

Form the ears by bending the coil back tightly on itself at one side of the head and passing back to the other side. Hold base of ears in place with several figure eight stitches as shown in Figure 6.9. The space inside the ears can be filled quite simply by working a separate thread over and under the outside edges until the centre is completely covered.

Now form the lip to the lid by coiling and stitching the core to the underside of the outer coil rather than around it as previously. Pass behind the ears making a complete circle. This will also leave the ears free to become the means whereby you lift the lid on and off your container. Slightly narrow the lip by working three more coils each on the inner edge of the previous coil. Taper the end of the core. Wind weft over core as before and when you reach the tapered end, stitch the weft round the end and the coil beneath it. The completed lip is thus formed by four rows of coils worked as a collar, Figure 6.10.

Make the cheeks by crocheting with white mohair:

> chain 4 and slip stitch into ring
> 8 double chain into centre of ring
> 2 double chain into each chain
> slip stitch to finish off.

Run a gathering thread around edge of cheek and pull up slightly. Stuff inside hollow with a length of white mohair, then stitch cheek in position. Make second cheek in same way.

The nose is embroidered in satin stitch worked between the cheeks. Decide whether you want to couch a mouth. The whiskers are made by stitching lengths of fishing line into the cheeks. Tie off black threads of pupils more securely, then cut ends.

Base: Once the lid has been made it is a simple matter to make the base. Working at the tapered end of the core, start coiling as described for the lid. Use Lazy Squaw stitch and build a flat coil with a diameter of 14 cm ($5\frac{1}{2}$ in). Now shape the sides and use figure eight stitch to hold coils in place. Build up sides, gradually narrowing work until lid fits snuggly in place. Cut the core, taper the end and finish off.

Having discovered how easy it is to build up shapes by coiling you might like to continue by adding feet and a tail.

Marmalade Moggy

A RANDOM DYED CREAM/GINGER WOOL has been used most effectively to crochet this little cat. The body consists of a lightly stuffed basic egg to which a crochet tail, ears and cheeks have been added. Facial features are embroidered. Marmalade Moggy would make a most unusual Easter gift for cat lovers. He could also very easily become a lion with a change of colour and the addition of loop stitches for a mane.

Materials

Patons Kismet (acrylic/mohair mixture) one 50 g ball
Few metres (yards) white mohair wool
Small amount of stuffing
Embroidery threads for nose, eyes and mouth
3.5 mm (9) crochet hook

Measurements

12.5 cm (5 in) tall

Tension

Normally when following pattern instructions for a garment you must work to the given tension if the article is to fit. This means of course that you will also use the named brand of wool. Since this is such a small, simple toy, tension is not so important. Consequently any other brand of slightly brushed wool would be suitable, just make sure that the hook is the right size to work easily. You will very quickly be able to see whether slightly more or less wool is needed to make Moggy. The finished size may well be very different.

Abbreviations

ch	chain
dc	double crochet
dec	decrease
Rnd	round
ss	slip stitch
yoh	yarn over hook

To decrease, insert hook into stitch, yoh and draw a loop through, insert hook into next stitch and draw a loop through. There should now be 3 loops on the hook. Wind yoh and draw through all three loops – one double crochet has been decreased.

To Make

Body: ch 4, ss in first ch to form ring

Rnd 1 ch 1, 8 dc in ring = 8 ch

Rnd 2 2 dc in each ch = 16 ch

Rnd 3 2 dc in each ch = 32 ch

Rnd 4 work even

Rnd 5 (7 dc then 2 dc in next ch) repeat 3 times = 36 ch

Rnds 6, 7, 8, 9 work even

Rnd 10 (8 dc then 2 dc in next ch) repeat 3 times = 40 ch

Rnds 11–16 work even

Rnd 17 (8 dc then dec in next 2 ch) repeat 3 times = 36 ch

Rnd 18 work even

Rnd 19 (7 dc then dec in next 2 ch) repeat 3 times = 32 ch

Rnd 20 work even

Rnd 21 (6 dc then dec in next 2 ch) repeat 3 times = 28 ch

Rnds 22, 24, 26 work even

Rnds 23, 25, 27 continue decreasing evenly

Rnd 28 work even – fill shape lightly with stuffing. Continue decreasing evenly until 4 ch remain. Fasten off and darn in end of wool.

Ears: Make a foundation row of 11 ch. Work 11 rows of 10 dc in each row and always work an extra ch for the turn at the beginning of each new row.

Fold ear in half to make a triangular shape. Oversew edges together then sew in place on head. Sew a few short tufts of white mohair wool inside the ear and trim to shape. Make second ear in same way.

Tail: Ch 11. Work 9 cm ($3\frac{1}{2}$ in) in dc, keeping edges even. Decrease 2 ch in last row = 8 ch. Change to white mohair and dc, 1 row. Dec in 2nd row, dc, 1 row, dec in 4th row = 6 ch. Fasten off. Sew sides of tail together and lightly stuff. Sew in position.

Cheeks: Ch 2. 8 dc into 2nd ch from hook. Work ss around edge. Sew in place with wrong side to outside, inserting a little stuffing to hold shape. Make second cheek in same way.

Face: Embroider a horizontal block of white satin stitches for the eye and a vertical block of black satin stitches for the pupil. Make second eye in same way. The nose is a triangular block of satin stitches between the cheeks on the upper curves, while the mouth is stem stitched beneath the cheeks.

Mittens of Kittens

MITTENS LEND THEMSELVES VERY easily to interpretation as Kittens and embroidered with their simple features they make wonderful starting points for puppets. Jungle Paws, with chain stitched pad marks, offer an opportunity for pouncing and creeping games, while Swiss darned eyes and smart whiskers make the quite superior Black Cats. Playful Kittens on the other hand are just that. Choose a tabby-like yarn then match it to a light and dark striped jumper and finish off with a swinging tail at the back.

Materials

Knitting needles size $3\frac{1}{4}$ mm (10) and 3 mm (11)

Jungle Paws

Crackerjack double knitting 1×40 g ball
few yards of contrast to work paws

Black Cats

Robin Reward double knitting 2×20 g balls
contrast wools to embroider face

Playful Kittens

Crackerjack double knitting, 1 ball each of cat colour, dark and light blue (this will make two pairs of mittens)
contrast wools to embroider face

Measurements

All mittens measure 12 cm ($4\frac{3}{4}$ in) round the hand.

Abbreviations

K	Knit
P	Purl
st(s)	stitch(es)
st st	stocking stitch
inc	increase
tog	together
sl	slip
psso	pass slip stitch over

To Make Up

All the mittens use a basic pattern which is given in full for Jungle Paws. The Black Cat variation has no shaping at the top while Playful Kittens have a separate little finger which becomes the arm of the cat.

Jungle Paws Right Hand Mitten

Using 3 mm needles, cast on 32 stitches and work 5 cm (2 in) of K1, P1 rib ending with a wrong side row.

Change to $3\frac{1}{4}$ mm needles and working in st st work 1 row K and 1 row P.

Thumb gusset

1st row K 16 sts, inc into next st, K1, inc into next st, K13.
2nd row P.
3rd row K.
4th row P.
5th row K16 sts, inc into next st, K3, inc into next st, K13.
Continue in this way, inc 1st on each side of the thumb gusset on every 4th row until there are 40 sts. Knit 3 more rows without shaping.
Next row K27 sts, turn and cast on 2 sts.
Next row P12 sts, turn and cast on 2 sts.
* Work 2.5 cm (1 in) on these 14 sts ending with a P row.
Next row K1 (K2, K2 tog) 3 times, K1.
Next row P.
Next row (K2 tog) 5 times, K1.
Cut off yarn and thread the end through the remaining sts, draw up and fasten off.
Sew thumb seam down to base. **
Pick up and K4 sts at the base of the thumb with right hand needle and K to end of row. Work on these 34 sts for 5 cm (2 in) ending with a P row.
Next row K2, (sl1, K1, psso, K10, K2 tog, K2) twice.
2nd, 4th and 6th row P.
3rd row K2, (sl1, K1, psso, K8, K2 tog, K2) twice.
5th row K2 (sl1, K1, psso, K6, K2 tog K2) twice.

7th row K2, (sl1, K1, psso, K4, K2 tog, K2) twice.
8th row P.
Cast off. *

Jungle Paws Left Hand Mitten

Work to match the Right Hand Mitten but reverse the position of the thumb gusset in the following way.

1st row K13 sts, inc into next st, K1, inc into next st, K16.
2nd row P.
3rd row K.
4th row P.
5th row K13 sts, inc into next st, K3, inc into next st, K16.
Continue in this way inc 1 st on each side of the gusset on every 4th row until 40 sts.
Work three more rows without any shaping.
Next row K23 sts, turn and cast on 2 sts.
Next row P12 sts, turn and cast on 2 sts.
Finish as for Right Hand Mitten, working from * to *.

To complete

Embroider chain stitch paws on the palm side of each mitten using Figure 6.11 as a guide. Work smaller pads first, then the large, central pad. Finally sew up side seam and across the top of the mitten.

Figure 6.11

Diagram of pad print for Jungle Paws mittens.

Black Cats Right Hand Mitten

Using black wool, work as for Jungle Paws Right Hand Mitten until **.

Pick up and K4 sts at the base of the thumb with right hand needle and K to end of row.

Work on these 34 sts for 7.5 cm (3 in) without shaping and end with a P row.
Cast off.

Sew up side seam of mitten and across top cast off edge. Turn mitten to right side and top stitch across each corner at an angle to form the ears. Figure 6.12 shows how to work Swiss darning and where to position the eyes. Keep a space of three stitches between the eyes. Work a satin stitch nose and stem stitch whiskers.

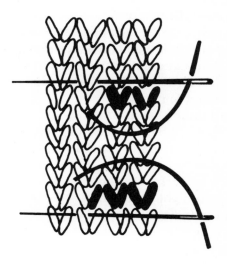

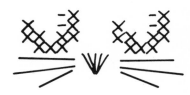

Figure 6.12

Swiss darning. This is a common form of embroidery used in knitting. It actually looks like a coloured pattern in stocking stitch without having the complications of knitting it in. Bring needle up through the centre of the appropriate stitch from back to front. Insert needle from right to left behind the stitch immediately above. Bring needle down through the centre of the original stitch. Repeat as necessary to complete pattern.

Black Cats Left Hand Mitten

Using black wool, work as for Jungle Paws Left Hand Mitten until thumb has been completed **, then finish as for Black Cats Right Hand Mitten.

Playful Kittens Right Hand Mitten

Using dark blue, work as for Jungle Paws Right Hand Mitten for 5 cm (2 in) rib.

Change to light blue and st st 2 rows.

Commence first 2 rows of thumb gusset. Change to dark blue and keeping increase for thumb gusset in order and colour change at every 4th row, work until 40 sts are on the needle.

Next row P in dark blue.

Change to light blue and st st 2 rows ***

Next row K27 sts, turn and cast on 2 sts.

Next row P12 sts, turn and cast on 2 sts.

Change to dark blue and st st 4 rows.

Change to cat colour and st st 2 rows.

Work last 3 rows of thumb as for Jungle Paws Right Hand Mitten.

Sew up thumb seam.

Pick up 4 stitches at base of thumb in light blue and K to end of row 34 sts.

Next row P.

Change to dark blue and st st 4 rows.

Change to light blue and st st 2 rows.

Next row K30, turn and cast on 1 st.

Next row P27, turn and cast on 1 st.

Change to cat colour and knit without shaping for 5 cm (2 in).

Cast off.

Sew 3 finger mitten across top and down side.

Little finger:

With light blue pick up 2 sts at base of mitten section and knit to end of row, 10 sts.

Next row P.

Change to dark blue and st st 4 rows.

Change to cat colour and st st 2 rows, ending with a P row.

Next row K1, (K2, K2 tog) twice, K1.

Next row P.

Next row (K2 tog) 4 times.

Complete as for thumb, and sew down side seam to wrist.

Playful Kittens Left Hand Mitten

Work as for Playful Kittens Right Hand Mitten until ***

Next row K23 sts, turn and cast on 2 sts.

Next row P12 sts, turn and cast on 2 sts.

Complete as for Playful Kittens Right Hand Mitten by changing to dark blue and st st 4 rows and so on.

Tail: Cut two lengths of cat colour, each 107 cm (42 in) long and thread needle on centrally. Sew through back of mitten, just above wrist section and leave both ends hanging. There should be four strands of 25.5 cm (10 in) on each side. Cut another two lengths and repeat so that there are 16 strands in all. Plait to make tail of required length. Tie off securely and trim ends.

Face: Work stem stitch in green wool for outline of eyes. Fill in centres with black satin stitches and pick out highlights with a single stitch of either lemon or white wool. Work satin stitch nose and straight stitches for mouth in a suitable colour.

CHAPTER SEVEN
The Big Cats

Lions, Tigers, Leopards and Jaguars are the Big Cats. They all roar while the smaller cats have more high-pitched voices. These cats also pause for breath between each purr whereas small cats purr almost continuously. The Puma, even though it is as large as a Leopard, cannot roar and is thus considered with the small cats. The Cheetah is an exception being the oddest of all the cats.

Tiger Cub

CHOOSE A SMALL PRINT TIGER FUR that contains white patches as well as ground colour and stripe. The head pattern is a smaller version of that used to make the Siamese kittens, while the body is a very simple lying pose. This cub makes an ideal mascot or pocket toy.

Materials

45.5 cm (18 in) by 30.5 cm (12 in) tiger fur
a pair of 12 mm eyes with slit pupil
small amount of stuffing
tan coloured embroidery thread for nose and mouth

Measurements

Cub sits 6 cm ($3\frac{1}{2}$ in) tall and 20 cm (8 in) long from tip of tail to front paws.

To Make Up -

Prepare a set of pattern pieces from the pattern grid (page 94). Cut a tail measuring 12 cm ($4\frac{3}{4}$ in) long by 6.5 cm ($2\frac{1}{2}$ in) wide. Place pattern on fur and cut so that the cub has white ear linings, pale underbody and darker stripes on upper body and back of head.

Follow instructions for Seal Point Siamese to make both the head and tail, then set aside while making the body.

Enclose finished tail in dart on upper body, then sew upper and lower body together leaving an opening at the back. It is easier to stitch the front paws if you slash between the legs and into the corners after sewing. Turn completed body right side out, stuff and close opening.

Ladder stitch head in position over the front legs. Embroider nose and mouth with tan coloured embroidery thread. Decide whether your Tiger Cub needs whiskers and work accordingly by following instructions given in Chapter One.

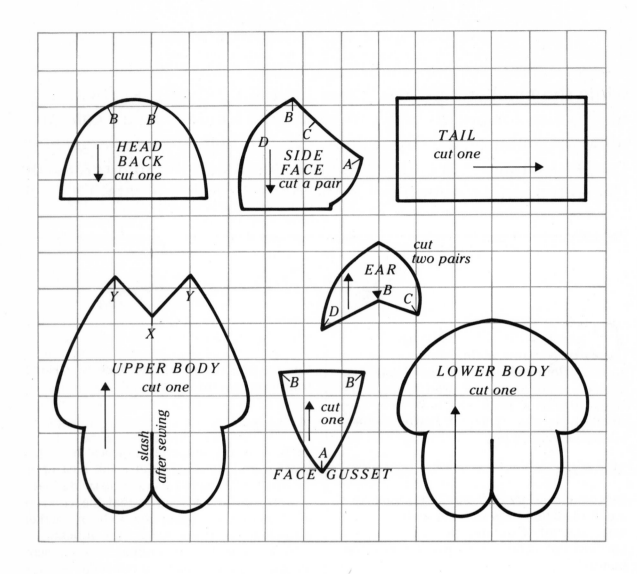

Pattern grid. **Tiger Cub** one **square**=2.5 cm (1 in)

Velvet Lion

LIONS ARE THE ONLY CATS WHICH normally live together in family groups at all times. Formerly spread over a much wider area, they are now found mostly in Africa south of the Sahara and in the Gir Forest on the north-western coast of India.

Materials

45.5 cm (18 in) velvet cushion square
112 g (4 oz) stuffing
25 g (1 oz) dark brown wool
small pieces of black and tan felt
black and white embroidery thread

Measurements

Lion stands 15 cm (6 in) tall and 23 cm (9 in) long.

To Make Up

Prepare a set of pattern pieces from the pattern grid (page 96) first, then cut Lion from the velvet. Cut a strip of velvet measuring 4.5 cm (1¾ in) wide by 6 cm (2¼ in) long for the tail.

Close the dart on the face by bringing Ys together and sewing from X down to Y. Make ears by sewing round outer edges only and turning right side out. With raw edges level, baste ears in position on the face, at either side of A. Now with right sides together sew back of head to face. Carefully cut a criss cross slit as marked in the centre of the back with the point of your scissors and use this opening to turn head right side out. Stuff firmly then bring points of slit together and catch in place.

Sew paired underbody pieces together from B to C, then sew centre back seam of main body from D to C and from B forward to the neck. Position underbody between legs and sew from B round legs to C on each side in turn. Clip corners and turn body right side out through neck opening. Stuff body firmly, then run a strong gathering thread round the neck pulling up sufficiently to roll raw edge over and out of sight.

Position head against neck and ladder stitch in place thus covering both openings. Cut two black felt circles for eyes and embroider white triangular highlights on each eye before hemming them in place. Cut a tan felt nose bridge and black felt nose. Hem these in place and finally work a stem stitch mouth.

Use a Quadframe set over 7 holes to make two 36 cm (14 in) lengths of curls. Sew these in place so that they completely cover the back of the head and frame the face, passing both sides of the ears. Alternatively make a fringe on the sewing machine or embroider loops for the mane.

Take the tail and fold each long side over towards the middle. Lay several lengths of wool along the centre with ends projecting beyond velvet at one end only. Ladder stitch folds together so that you make a tube with wool in centre as the filling. Sew tail to body and trim tassel to required shape and length.

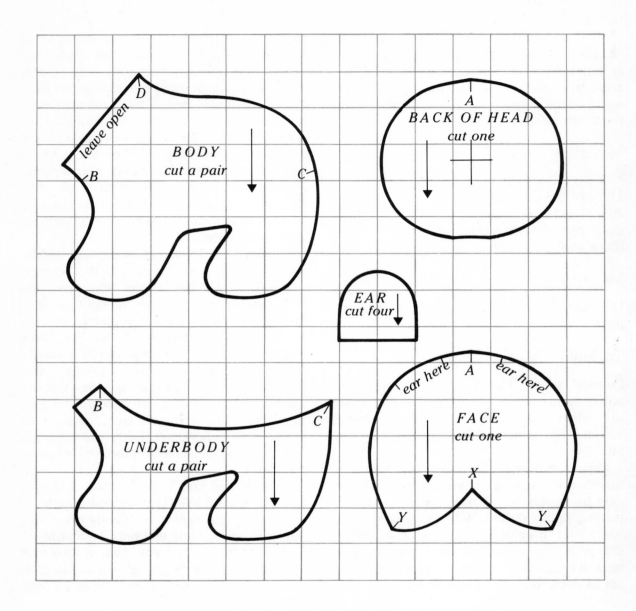

Pattern grid. **Velvet Lion one square=2.5 cm (1 in)**

The Big Cats (opposite)
Tiger Tiger, Tiger Cub, Velvet Lion.

Tiger Tiger

TIGERS, THE LARGEST OF ALL THE big cats and the only true striped species, have a range in nature that extends from China and Siberia in the north to Bali in the south and Persia in the west. With such a wide range it is only natural that the Tiger shows variation in both size and appearance in different areas. Tigers of the north are generally larger and paler than those of the south. White Tigers are not true albinos but animals with reduced dark pigmentation having dark brown stripes on almost white fur, ice-blue eyes and pink noses and pads to their paws. Sadly, many populations of these graceful animals are seriously endangered.

Materials

61 cm (24 in) by 137 cm (54 in) wide simulated tiger fur preferably with no white ground colour
25 cm (10 in) by 38 cm (15 in) long unpolished white fur
pair of 21 mm yellow safety eyes
yellow and black felt for eye backings
Peri-Lusta Floran tan thread for nose
plain biscuit colour fur for muzzle
510 g (1lb 2 oz) stuffing
fishing line for whiskers

Measurements

61 cm (24 in) tall

To Make Up

Prepare a set of card patterns from the pattern grids (pages 98 and 99). Examine the tiger fur closely and determine where the vertical black stripes occur as opposed to lighter coloured areas with horizontal black patterning. The pattern pieces need to be placed carefully on the fur so that the back has

Tail Piece (opposite)
From the back to the front: *Hamish, Flora, Duncan, Margaret.*

a central spine of black which continues from the head down the back and along the length of the tail. The head gusset should also be dark. Generally the fronts of the limbs are lighter in colour as is the surround of the chest.

Start by making the body. Sew the chest to front side on each side in turn from E to F. Fold front in half lengthways and bring lower edges together. Now sew from G through F to H. Make the three darts on the body back by bringing Ys together and sewing from X to Y in turn. Set aside and make the arms and legs.

With right sides together sew a pair of arm pieces together leaving the top open. Clip between claws, then turn arm right side out and stuff nearly to the top. Press open edges together and baste arm to front of body with raw edges level. Make second arm in the same way and again baste in position.

Stretch out inner curve of foot and with right sides together place against lower edge of leg matching BAB and sew. Fold leg in half lengthways and sew centre back seam from C at ankle through B to D at top of leg. Run an easing thread around toes and pull up, adjusting fullness until sole fits opening. Baste sole in place being careful to tuck fur in on the curves. Turn completed leg right side out and stuff nearly to the top. Press opening flat with seam at centre back and baste raw edges together. Place leg against body front and with raw edges level, sew in place. Make a second leg in the same way and baste in position.

With right sides together sew front body to back. Start on the outside edge of a leg and continue up the side, around the neck projection and down to the outside edge of the second leg. Keep limbs folded out of the way so as not to catch them in the seams. Turn body right side out and stuff firmly. Close opening behind legs, enclosing more stuffing in the seating area as necessary.

Determine stroke of pile on tail then fold it in half lengthways and sew across the bottom rounding off the corners and up the length. Trim away excess fur on curves and turn tail

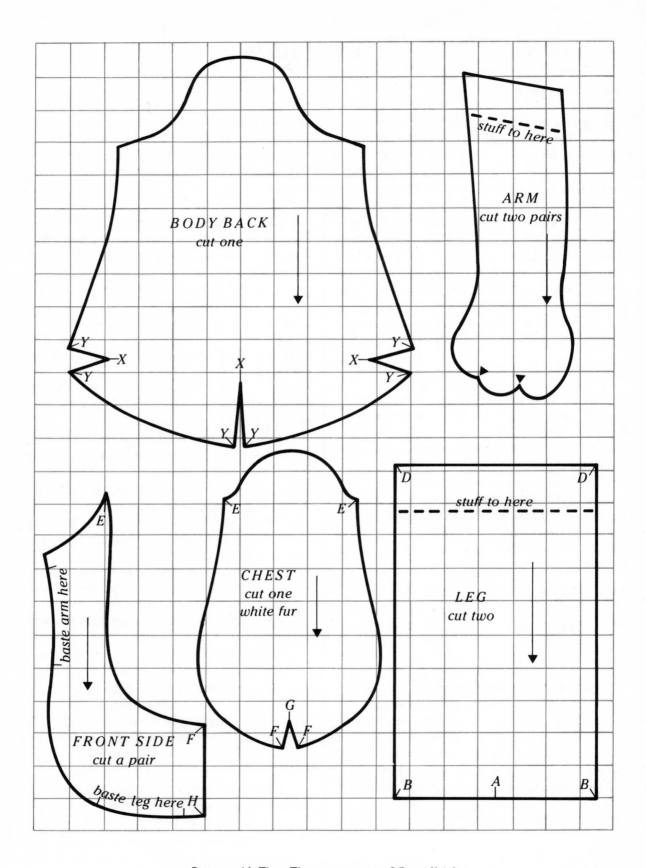

BODY BACK
cut one

ARM
cut two pairs

stuff to here

Y X Y X X Y Y Y

CHEST
cut one
white fur

E E

D D

stuff to here

LEG
cut two

E

baste arm here

FRONT SIDE F
cut a pair

baste leg here H

G
F F

B A B

Pattern grid. **Tiger Tiger one square=2.5 cm (1 in)**

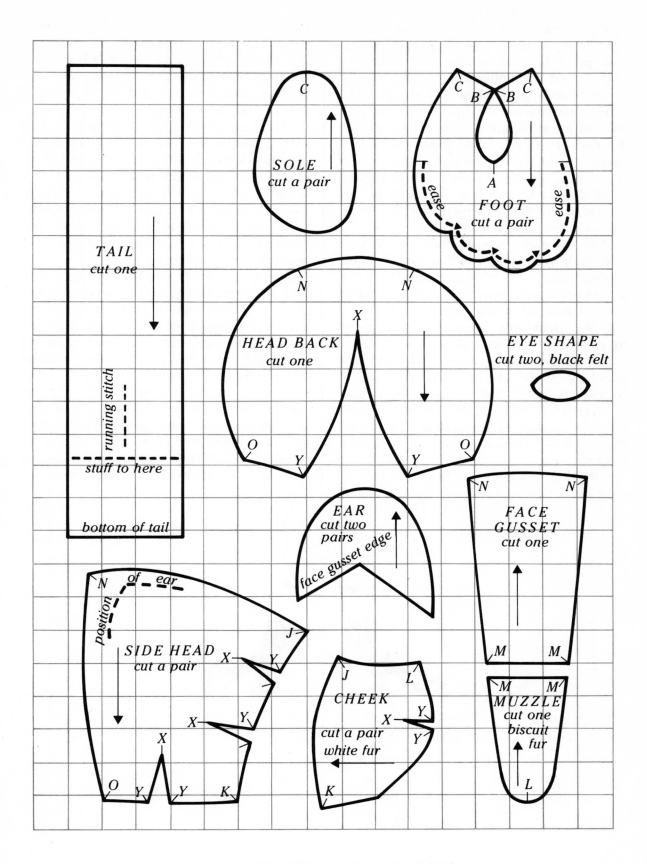

Pattern grid. **Tiger Tiger** one square=2.5 cm (1 in)

right side out. Push a small amount of stuffing right down to the bottom to provide weight, then press tail flat so that the seam lies centrally on the underside. Using a strong double thread, work a few inches of running stitch centrally on the upper surface, just ahead of the stuffing. Pull up on thread so that the end of the tail curls. Fasten off when satisfied with the appearance. Turn in raw edges at top of tail and baste together. Ladder stitch tail to backside at the head of the central seating dart. Set completed body aside and work on the head.

Make the darts on head back, cheeks and side heads by bringing Y to Y in each case and sewing from X to Y. With right sides together sew cheek to side head from J to K for both sides of the head making sure that you have a left and right side. Now sew both sides together from L to neck at K.

Sew nose gusset (muzzle) to face gusset matching M to M on each side. Insert completed gusset between side heads and sew from L to N on each side in turn. Sew head back to completed front from O on side through N–N to O on the other side. Turn head right side out.

Cut yellow felt circles to fit on the back of each eye. These will enhance the eye colour which would otherwise become dull against the fur. Hold felt in place with a spot of glue. Cut black felt eye shapes and thread one on to the back of each eye then fix completed eye units in place being careful not to twist the black felt in the process.

Stuff head firmly. Run a strong gathering thread around the neck opening but do not pull up completely. Lower the head on to the neck projection of the body. This acts as a strengthening support and should help to hold the head in place. When satisfied with both the fit and position, pull up on the gathering thread and ladder stitch the head securely to the body.

Sew ears together in pairs then turn right side out. Baste raw edges together and at this stage clean out trapped fur from the curved seams. Position ears on head so that the forward edge lies along the gusset seam and the rest of the ear lies along the line marked on the pattern.

Embroider nose on very edge of the muzzle by working a broad triangular block of satin stitches down on to the cheeks. Embroider a mouth on to the cheeks and finally add a set of whiskers on each side, using a stronger fishing line than that used for any of the kittens.

CHAPTER EIGHT
Tail Piece

Mice figure so prominently in the life of cats that it would be impossible not to let them have a place of their own in the book. These paired mice are in Scottish dress with Duncan and Margaret wearing brightly coloured kilts whilst Hamish and Flora are in darker colours. To complete the outfits the lads have a sporran and tam-o'-shanter and the lassies have a blouse and plaid.

Duncan and Hamish

DUNCAN WEARS THE GREEN waistcoat and matching tartan but in every other respect is similar to Hamish as both mice are made in exactly the same way.

Materials

The following materials make one mouse:
25 cm (10 in) by 69 cm (27 in) wide honey coloured fur
112 g (4 oz) stuffing
a pair of black domed buttons or beads for eyes
small ball of flesh coloured wool
23 cm (9 in) square flesh coloured felt
approximately 15 pipe cleaners
small piece of tartan for kilt and tam-o'-shanter
felt for waistcoat
snap fasteners, buttons and safety pin
small pieces of white fur and white felt
red wool for pompom
15 cm (6 in) black tape

Measurements

Duncan and Hamish MacMousie stand approximately 23 cm (9 in) tall.

To Make Up

Make a set of card patterns from the pattern grid. Measurements for the tail, kilt and tam-o'-shanter are given in the instructions. All pattern pieces include a 6 mm ($\frac{1}{4}$ in) seam allowance except for the ears and tail.

Body: Start by making the head darts on each side body, matching X to X first then sewing Y to X. Insert front gusset matching A to A and B to B and sew each side in turn. Sew both side bodies together from X working forward through C to D. The opening between ADA is for turning the completed body right side out. Finish centre back seam by sewing down body from X to B. Turn completed skin right side out and stuff, paying particular attention to rounding out the cheeks and keeping the neck firm. Ladder stitch the neck opening.

Make the nose by running a gathering thread round the edge of the felt circle. Start to pull up the thread forming a hollow into which you can insert a small ball of stuffing. Pull up tight on thread and fasten off securely. Using a pencil, push in the head at C forming a socket that will take the stalk of the nose. Sew nose securely to head.

Position eyes and sew in place with strong thread. Place a felt ear lining on the wrong side

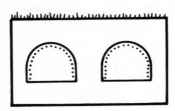

Figure 8.1

Diagram of felt ear linings top stitched to the wrong side of the fur and completed ears sewn in position on the head.

of a piece of fur and either machine or stab stitch round the curved edge. Cut away excess fur fabric and trim to shape with sharp embroidery scissors. Clean sewing line on fur side by stroking fur with a needle to raise the pile. Fold ear in half and whip base together. Position ear just in front of head dart and sew in place, spreading the base open to make the ears more petal shaped, Figure 8.1.

The hands and feet of MacMousie are made by winding wool over pipe cleaners which can then be bent into the shape of fingers and toes. Wind a single layer of wool along the length of a pipe cleaner then bend it in the middle to make two fingers. Wrap each finger with wool, then make another set of two fingers in the same way. The four fingers can now be placed together, side by side, and the hand formed by wrapping several layers of wool over the pipe cleaners, building up the required shape. Make a second hand in the same way, Figure 8.2.

Hem a single fold along the wrist edge of the arm, then bring the straight edges together and sew them on the wrong side making a centre back seam. Turn arm right side out and insert hand into arm, stitch securely in place. Stuff arm and finish by running a gathering thread around the top opening and pulling up before fastening off, Figure 8.3. Position arm on side of body in required position and ladder stitch in place. Finish the other arm in the same way. Gently bend fingers to give a pleasing shape.

Prepare a foot by winding wool along each of two pipe cleaners, as you did for the hands,

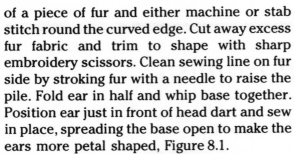

Figure 8.2

Diagram showing how fingers are made from pipe cleaners, bound with wool and then bent into shape to form a hand for MacMousie.

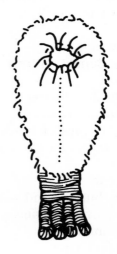

Figure 8.3

Arm viewed from the back showing centre back seam and gathers pulled up to enclose stuffing.

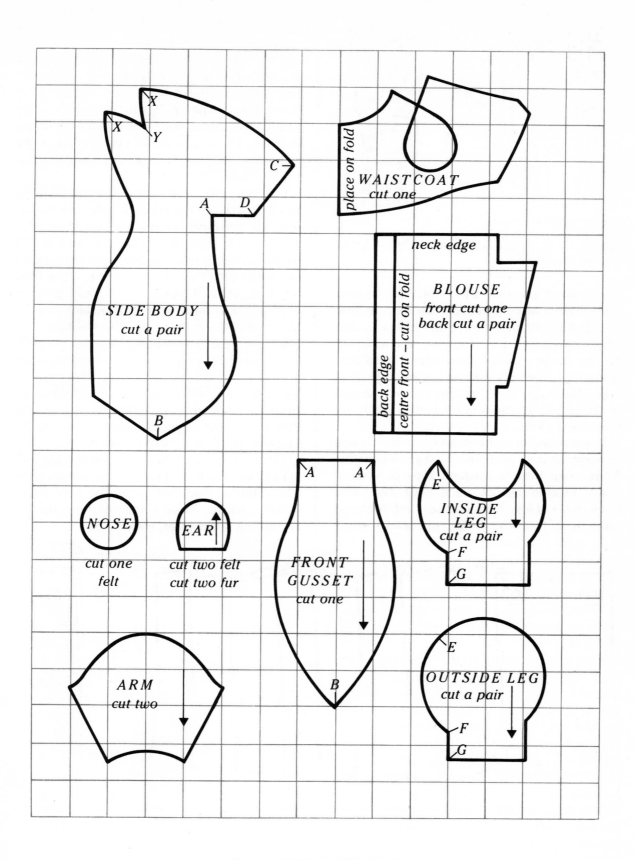

Pattern grid. Duncan, Margaret,
Hamish and Flora one square=2.5 cm (1 in)

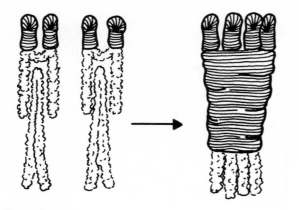

Figure 8.4

Diagram showing how toes are formed and then bound with wool to form a foot.

thus making four toes. Place toes side by side and add two more pipe cleaners, bent in half, to the base of the toes. This increases the length of the foot. Bind the pipe cleaners with several layers of wool, building up the shape of the foot. The very ends of the pipe cleaners may be left uncovered as they will be inserted in the leg. Make the second foot in the same way, Figure 8.4.

Place together right sides of an inside and outside leg, matching F to F and sew down this front seam from E through F to G. Make a single hem along the ankle edge, then sew back seam of leg. Turn leg right side out and push foot into the ankle opening leaving

approximately 6 cm showing. Sew foot securely in place then bend it forward. Stuff leg, run a gathering thread around the top of the leg, draw up the opening and fasten off. Make second leg in the same way checking that you have a pair rather than two. Place legs against the side of the body and ladder stitch in place. Variations in the positioning of the legs will enable you to make taller and shorter MacMousies.

Cut a piece of flesh coloured felt measuring 23 cm (9 in) by 4 cm (1½ in) for the tail. Fold it in half lengthways and sew a tapered tail. Trim away excess felt close to the sewing line. Fill the cavity of the tail with several pipecleaners or wire to give it rigidity. Sew tail in place then bend it at foot level to lie on ground. MacMousie is thus supported by feet and tail which effectively increases the stability.

Kilt: Cut a piece of tartan 53 cm (21 in) wide by 12 cm (5 in) long. Fold the lower long edge over twice and make a narrow hem. Neaten top long edge with machine zigzag stitch or whip by hand, then fold over to wrong side making kilt the required length for the body. Machine the fold to hold in place.

Make a narrow pleat on the short edge that is to be the top flap of the kilt. Secure pleat by top stitching then withdraw the threads to make a fringe. Make a narrow hem on the remaining short edge, Figure 8.5.

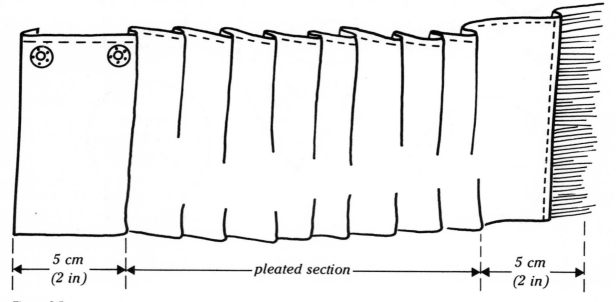

5 cm (2 in) ——pleated section—— 5 cm (2 in)

Figure 8.5

Kilt showing construction of front wraps and pleated section.

Pleat kilt into nine or ten central folds leaving 5 cm (2 in) free on either side to form the front wrap. Adjust folds as necessary according to the plumpness of your mouse. Machine across waist edge to hold pleats in place, then iron folds under a damp cloth to make them permanent. Sew on two snap fasteners at waist edge of wrap. Place kilt on mouse and finish dressing with a small safety pin on the flap.

Sporran: Using the ear pattern as a template cut one white fur and one white felt piece. Work two tassels on the front of the fur piece with black sewing thread. Oversew felt to back of fur piece then catch stitch sporran in place on front of kilt.

Waistcoat: Back the felt waistcoat with iron-on Vilene to give it more strength. Sew shoulder seams by overlapping front to back. Sew button on front opening and then either work a button hole or sew on a snap fastener under the button to close the waistcoat.

Tam-o'-shanter: Cut a 15 cm (6 in) diameter circle of tartan, then make a 6 cm (2½ in) slash into the circle from the outside edge. Work a

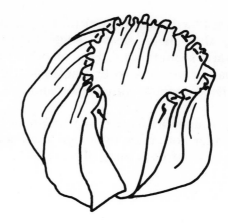

Figure 8.6

Tam-o'-shanter showing slash and gathered edge.

gathering thread around the outside edge and pull up to measure approximately 14 cm (5½ in), Figure 8.6. Sew a length of black tape to the right side of the gathers, then place slashed edges together and seam. Turn under black tape to wrong side and hem in place. Make a small red wool pompom and stitch on top, centrally. Arrange tam-o'-shanter on head and catch in place with a few stitches.

Margaret and Flora

THE LASSIES WEAR WHITE BLOUSES trimmed with lace jabots and have plaids fastened on their left shoulders.

Materials

As given for Hamish and Duncan with an additional piece of white cotton to make the blouse
15 cm (6 in) white lace for jabot
metallic button and small safety pin to make brooch

Measurements

Margaret and Flora MacMousie stand approximately 20 cm (8 in) tall.

To Make Up

Make a set of card patterns from the pattern grid. Measurements are given in the instructions for making the plaid. All pattern pieces include a 6 mm (¼ in) seam allowance except for the ears and tail.

Body: Follow the instructions given for making up Duncan and Hamish. Position legs slightly higher on the side body to make the mouse shorter than her companion. A larger seam allowance will also help to make a smaller body if you want to vary the size further without reducing the pattern.

Kilt: Adjust the length of the kilt making it shorter. The girls do not have a sporran on their kilts.

Blouse: Sew backs to front on the shoulder seam, then hem sleeve edges and sew underarm seam to waist. Hem all other edges and gather up neck to fit MacMousie. Close back neck opening with a hook and eye.

Jabot: Gather a 15 cm (6 in) length of lace, turn under both ends to neaten, then sew in place on front neck edge of blouse.

Plaid: Cut an 18 cm (7 in) square of tartan fabric. Work a row of stay stitching round all four sides about 12 mm ($\frac{1}{2}$ in) in from the edge, then withdraw threads to fringe the edges. Fold plaid in half diagonally and sew a metallic button in place as a brooch. Sew a brooch pin or small safety pin behind the button and on the inside of the plaid. Drape plaid over left shoulder and pin in place with the brooch.

Index

American block patchwork patterns,   54, **55**
Appliqué patterns:
   Sunbonnet Sue,   59–60:
   The Owl and the Pussycat,   62–4
Aunt Sukey's choice
   block pattern (Puss in Boots),   54, **55**

Belt, Pompom Puss,   80–1;
   template,   **81**
Big Cats:
   Tiger Cub,   93, **94;**
   Tiger, Tiger,   97–100, **98, 99;**
   Velvet Lion,   95, **96**
Black Cats mittens,   91
Block patterns,   54, **55**
Blouse,   106
Blue Kitten,   26;
   body pattern,   **26**
Blue-eyed White Shorthair Kitten,   19–22;
   pattern guide,   **21**
Boots and Tabby,   82–5;
   wire frames,   **82, 83**
Boxes, fabric covered,   73–6;
   lacing,   **74;**
   rosettes,   **75**

Canvas embroidery,   76–9;
   Cat in Clover chart,   **77**
Cat and Mice block pattern,   **55**
Cat bed,   28–9
Cat in Clover slip-on cover,   76–9;
   chart,   **77**
Cathedral Window pin cushion,   43–4
Cat's Cradle cushion,   52–4;
   template,   53
   block,   **54**
Claws block pattern,   **55**
Coiled Cat,   86–8
Cat quilt, Daisy Chain,   59–60;
   pattern grid,   **61**
Cotton wool pouch,   70
Crochet cat, Marmalade Moggy,   88–9
Cross stitch embroidery,   69–72, **71;**
   Cotton Wool Pouch,   70;
   Dorothy Bag,   70;
   Tissue Box Cover,   70, 72, **72;**
   Wet Ones cover,   70
Cushions: Cat's Cradle,   52–4;
   Puss in the Corner,   50–2
Cushion, Puss in the Corner,   50–2;
   templates, **51**
Cushion, Cat's cradle,   52–4;
   template,   **53;**
   block,   **54**
Cut woolly ball technique,   80–5;
   template,   **81**

Daisy Chain cot quilt,   59–60;
   pattern grid,   **61**
Dorothy bag,   70
Dresden Plate egg cosies,   44;
   template,   **44**
Duffel bag, Egyptian cat,   56–8;
   templates,   **57;**
   diagram,   **58**
Duncan and Hamish MacMousie,   101–5;
   pattern grid,   **103**

Ears,   20, **20,** 23, 38, 81, **87,** 100, 102, **102**
Ebony Oriental Shorthair Kitten,   28;
   pattern grid,   **27**
Egg cosies, Dresden Plate,   44;
   template,   **44**
Egyptian Cat duffel bag,   56–8;
   templates,   **57;**
   diagram,   **58**
Embroidered boxes,   73–6
Embroidery stitches: cross stitch,   69, **71;**
   French Knots,   **76;**
   Swiss darning,   **91;**
   tent stitch,   78, **79;**
   whipped spider's web,   **76**
Eyes,   19–20, 24, **86,** 95, 100

Fabric covered boxes,   73–6
Feet and hands,   102, 104, **102, 104**
French Knot stitch,   **76**

Gingham Collection, The,   69–72;
   cross stitch chart,   **71**

Half Blood Knots,   33, **33**

Jabot,   106
Jaguar rosettes,   **75**
Japanese Bobtail Kitten,   24–5;
   body pattern,   **25;**
   pattern grid,   **25**
Jungle Paws mittens,   90–1, **91**
Just Good Friends pillow,   66;
   pattern grid,   **67**

Kilt,   104–5, **104,** 105
Kit bag, Siamese,   48–50;
   templates,   **49**
Kitten mittens: Black Cats,   91;
   Jungle paws,   90–1, **91;**
   Playful Kittens,   92
Kittens: Blue,   26;
   Blue-eyed White Shorthair,   19–22;
   Ebony Oriental Shorthair,   28;
   Japanese Bobtail,   24–5;
   Red Colourpoint Longhair,   22–3;

Red Tabby Shorthair, 23–4;
    Seal Point Siamese, 26–8
Kitty corner block pattern, **55**
Knitted mittens, 90–2

Ladder stitch, **22**
Lazy Squaw stitch, **86**
Leopard rosettes, **75**
Log Cabin pot holder, 41–2;
    layout, **42**

MacMousies, 101–6
Margaret and Flora MacMousie, 105–6
Marmalade Moggy crochet cat, 88–9
Mascot, Tiger Cub, 93, **94**
Mice, 101–6
Miss Pussy Willow, 36–40;
    pattern grids, **37, 39**
Mitring of corners, **47,** 48;
    box, 74
Mittens: Black Cats, 91;
    Jungle Paws, 90–1, **91;**
    Playful Kittens, 92

Nose, 20, **20**, 22, **22**, 30, 38, **38**, 100, 101

Owl and Pussycat appliqué pattern, 62–4;
    templates, **63**

Patchwork, 41–58, **62**
Pincushion, Cathedral Window, 43–4
Plaid, 106
Playful Kittens mittens, 92
Playful Persians pillow, 68;
    pattern grid, **67**
Pompom Puss belt, 80–1;
    template, **81**
Pot holder, Log Cabin, 41–2;
    layout, **42**
Puss in Boots block pattern, **55**
Puss in the Corner block pattern, **55**
Puss in the Corner scatter cushion, 50–2;
    templates, **51, 52**

Quadframe, 82, 83, 95
Quilt: Catch Us If You Can, 45–8;
    arrangement of patches, **45;**
    templates, **46, 47;**
    Daisy chain, 59–60;
    pattern grid, **61**

Quilted pillows: Just Good Friends, 66;
    Playful Persians, 68;
    Sleepy Head, 65
Quilting, 60

Red Colourpoint Longhair Kitten, 22–3;
    pattern grid, **21**
Red Self Shorthair Kitten, 24
Red Tabby Shorthair Kitten, 23–4;
    body pattern, **23**
Rosettes, jaguar and leopard, **75**

Scatter cushion, Puss in the Corner, 50–2;
    templates, **51, 52**
Seal Point Siamese Kitten, 26–8;
    pattern grid, **27**
Silver grey cat chart, **77**
Sleepy Head pillow, 65;
    pattern grid, **67**
Slip-on cover, Cat in Clover, 76–9;
    chart, **77**
Sporran, 105
Sunbonnet Sue appliqué pattern, 59–60
Sweet Dreams cat bed, 28–9;
    cutting diagram, **29**
Sweet-smelling pillows, 65–8
Swiss darning, **91**

Tabby, 85
Tabitha, 34–6;
    pattern grid, **35**
Tail, 20, **22**, 25, 34, 95, 97, 100, 104
Tam-o'-shanter, 105, **105**
Tent stitch, 78, **79**
Tiger Cub, 93;
    pattern grid, **94**
Tiger, Tiger, 97–100;
    pattern grids, **98, 99**
Tissue box cover, 70, 72, **72**
Tom, 30–3;
    pattern grids, **31, 32**

Velvet lion, 95;
    pattern grid, **96**

Waistcoat, 105
Wet Ones cover, 70
Whipped spider's web stitch, **76**
Whiskers, 20–2, 33, **33,** 93, 100
Wool cats, 80–92

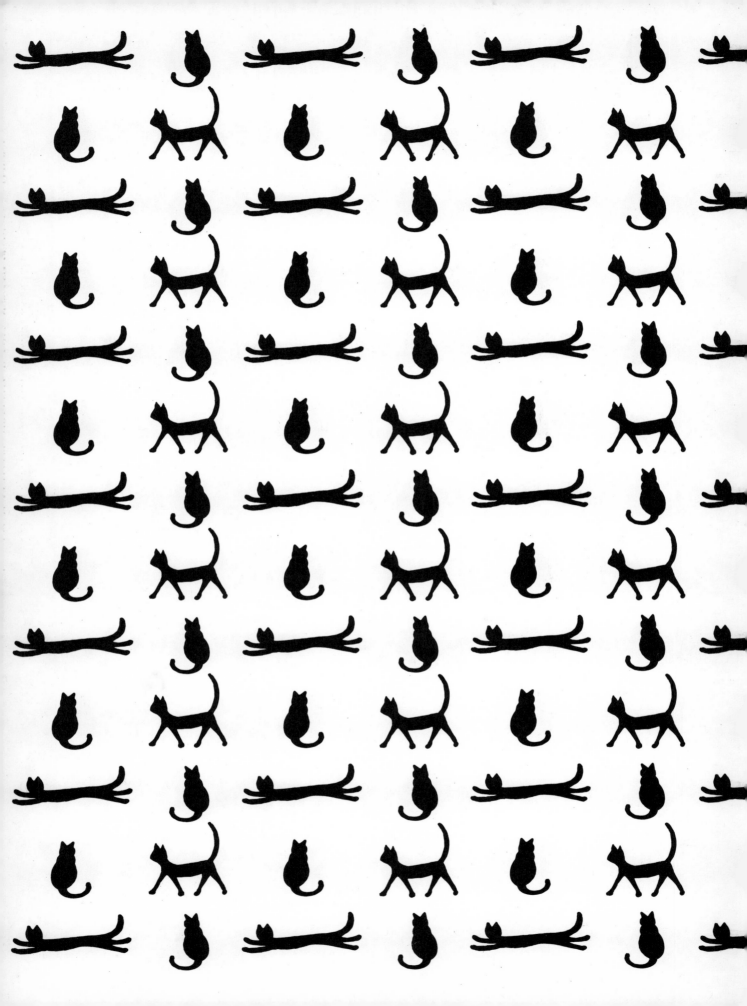